Type 2 Diabetes

An Integrative Medicine Treatment Program

A SPECIAL REPORT FROM THE EDITORS OF

Dr. Andrew Weil's Self Healing

Self Healing is Dr. Andrew Weil's monthly health newsletter, which is published by MSX, Inc., 42 Pleasant St., Watertown MA 02472; *www.drweilselfhealing.com*; (617) 926-0200. For subscription information, please call (800) 523-3296.

ISBN 0–9706414–9–4

Printed in the United States of America

WRITER AND RESEARCHER Jessica Cerretani

MEDICAL EDITOR Andrew Weil, MD

EDITORS Cari Nierenberg | Dan Fields

EDITORIAL INTERNS Erin Morin | Einav Ornan

ART DIRECTION & DESIGN Mary Lynch

PUBLISHER Janesse T. Bruce

CIRCULATION Shirley Barry | Devin McCloskey | Barbara Hamwey

PRODUCTION Mandy Stone-DerHagopian

Cover photograph: Dex Images, Inc./CORBIS

Table of Contents

Introduction

Dear Reader,

Welcome to *Type 2 Diabetes: An Integrative Medicine Treatment Program*. Whether you've just been diagnosed with type 2 diabetes or have been struggling with high blood sugar levels for years, you're probably looking for advice on keeping the disease under control and staying healthy. Perhaps you've wondered whether sugar is safe to eat, if you'll need to use insulin, or whether any dietary supplements can help keep blood sugar low.

That's why the editors of my newsletter and I have created this book. Once known as "adult-onset diabetes" because it was rarely seen in younger people, type 2 diabetes is now epidemic in this country and around the world. Alarmingly, experts predict that global rates of the disease will more than double by the year 2030, and more and more young adults, teens, and even children are being diagnosed. I think this is due in large part to the rising numbers of people who are overweight or obese, to increased consumption of poor-quality, refined carbohydrates, and to a lack of exercise.

Even if you already have diabetes, there's much you can do to delay its progression and keep it from worsening. Although some cases of diabetes do require conventional treatment with oral medications or insulin, they can also greatly benefit from a variety of lifestyle changes involving diet, physical activity, and weight control, as well as stress reduction, supplements, and other natural measures. It's my firm belief that many people with diabetes can put the disease into remission with these strategies as well. Known as integrative medicine, this approach aims to take advantage of the body's innate healing capacity, rather than just treating the symptoms of disease.

This clear, in-depth report offers a comprehensive integrative treatment program for diabetes that's designed to help lower your blood sugar and prevent complications of the disease. The treatments, supplements, dietary measures, and other approaches discussed in this report are the best researched, the most popular, and the most asked about. We've also talked with a variety of experts—from an endocrinologist to an exercise physiologist—to bring you the best information about diabetes treatment. As the medical editor of this report, I've reviewed all the advice offered here to make sure it's based both on the latest research and my experience treating patients with diabetes.

Type 2 Diabetes: An Integrative Medicine Treatment Program covers many diverse aspects of treating this condition. You'll be introduced to herbs and supplements that may help reduce the amount of diabetes medication you take. You'll also learn about lifestyle strategies—the best dietary advice for people with diabetes, how physical activity and relaxation techniques can lower blood sugar, techniques to relieve stress that can worsen the disease, and tips for coping with it from day to day. We've also included plenty of practical "Try This" activities so you can start taking advantage of the program right away. Plus, there's a resource guide and selected references, to help you stay informed long after you've finished reading this book.

I hope that these pages bring you a new sense of personal control to manage diabetes, and that it becomes a trusted reference that you can turn to for valuable medical advice whenever you need it.

To your good health,

Andrew Weil, MD

CHAPTER ONE

Diabetes 101

B eing told you're really sweet is usually a good thing, but not when you hear it from your doctor in reference to your blood. That means the sugar in your blood is too high—it's a sign that you may have diabetes.

You're not alone. More than 18 million Americans have diabetes, mainly type 2, and more than a third of them don't even know it. About the same number are estimated to have prediabetes, a condition that puts them at high risk for the disease. Those numbers are expected to increase substantially in the next few decades, as both adults and children become increasingly heavier and inactive, two major risk factors. There's no doubt that type 2 diabetes is an epidemic, and a serious one at that: It's a chronic disease that needs constant monitoring and possibly lifelong medication; it can have whole-body effects and widespread complications.

Fortunately, you can take action to control your diabetes, and you don't need to rely solely on conventional medications. Lifestyle approaches like exercise, diet, weight control, and stress reduction are so effective at controlling blood sugar levels that you should follow them even if you are taking diabetes drugs, says Mark Feinglos, MD, chief of endocrinology at Duke University Medical Center in Durham, North Carolina. Such lifestyle measures may help you and your doctor lower your dose of medication or even eliminate it. An integrative medicine treatment program for diabetes can also include certain vitamins, minerals, herbs, and other dietary supplements. Followed closely, these measures can also help reduce the risk of diabetes complications. Before you learn about these treatments, though, you need to first understand diabetes and how it occurs.

"A journey of a thousand miles begins with a single step."

LAO TZU

What's Going On in Your Body?

Most of the food you eat is broken down into the simple sugar glucose and released into the bloodstream. Glucose is what your body uses for fuel. Just as your car needs gasoline to run, your body relies on glucose to give your muscles, brain, and other organs the energy they need to keep working. To do this job, glucose needs to get out of your bloodstream and into cells.

Your pancreas (a large organ behind your stomach) releases a hormone called insulin, which helps move glucose from your blood into your cells. When insulin attaches to insulin receptors on cells, the cells recognize glucose and let it in.

In one form of diabetes called type 1 diabetes (see box on page 9), the immune system attacks the pancreas until it can no longer produce enough insulin to move glucose into cells. Instead, it stays in the blood, leading to high blood sugar levels. Symptoms of the disease, like increased thirst, urination, and fatigue, often appear suddenly, most commonly in children and young adults.

The process works differently in people with type 2 diabetes, although the outcome is similar. (Type 2 diabetes is by far the more common form and the one this book will discuss. When you see the word "diabetes" in this guide, it refers to type 2.) In people with this disease, the pancreas produces enough insulin, but, for reasons that are still unclear, cells start ignoring it, a problem known as insulin resistance. Of people who have insulin resistance, only some go on to develop full-blown diabetes. This happens when the pancreas works overtime, producing more and more insulin to get cells to respond. Eventually, the pancreas gets exhausted and can't make as much insulin as it once did. Glucose builds up in the blood and, just as with type 1 diabetes, your body can't get enough glucose inside cells to use as fuel.

The symptoms of type 2 diabetes (like frequent thirst and urination and feeling tired all the time) can be similar to those of type 1, but they may take much longer to develop. Left unchecked, though, such high levels of blood sugar can cause long-term damage to your blood vessels and nerves, resulting in problems with your eyes, skin, limbs, heart, kidneys, brain, and other body parts (see Chapter Eight).

Diabetes: What's Your Type?

There are three main kinds of diabetes—type 1, type 2, and gestational diabetes. Type 2 diabetes is the most common form, accounting for 95 percent of diabetes cases. Here are some other key differences between these types:

	Type 1 (formerly called juvenile diabetes)	Type 2 (formerly called adult-onset diabetes)	Gestational
Who gets it?	Usually people under age 30. You're at higher risk for type 1 diabetes if another family member has it. It's an autoimmune disease, but the exact causes are unknown.	Mostly people over age 50, but children and younger adults are increasingly being diagnosed. More likely in people who are overweight or obese, inactive, have a family history of diabetes or a personal history of gestational diabetes, or who are African American, Native American, Pacific Islander, Latino, or Asian.	About 4 percent of pregnant women, usually in the fifth or sixth month of pregnancy. Women who are African American, Native American, Pacific Islander, Latino, or Asian, or who have a family history of diabetes, are at higher risk.
What's the process?	The pancreas loses its ability to make insulin, as the immune system destroys its insulin-producing cells.	Cells become resistant to insulin.	Pregnancy hormones somehow make the body unable to produce and use all the insulin it needs.
Is it preventable?	No, but some researchers believe that it may be triggered by exposure to cow's milk during infancy in genetically susceptible people.	Yes. Diet, exercise, and maintaining a healthy weight can help prevent it.	No, but you may be able to prevent gestational diabetes from becoming type 2 diabetes by following the same preventive measures for that disease.
Autoimmune disorder?	Yes	No	No
What are the symptoms?	Symptoms often occur suddenly and include increased thirst, hunger, and urination, as well as weight loss, blurred vision, and extreme fatigue.	Symptoms develop gradually over years but are similar to those of type 1 diabetes. Some people have no symptoms.	Excessive thirst and urination, although most women are diagnosed before they develop symptoms.
Will you need to take insulin?	Yes. People with type 1 diabetes must inject themselves with insulin every day.	Maybe. Some people with severe type 2 diabetes may need to use supplemental insulin, but most people don't.	Only in severe cases. Most of the time, gestational diabetes can be managed with dietary changes alone and has no negative effects on the baby.
Will it go away?	No	Not permanently, although lifestyle measures may put many cases into complete remission.	Yes, typically within a few months of giving birth. But you have an increased risk of developing gestational diabetes with your next pregnancy and up to a 60 percent higher risk of developing type 2 diabetes later in life.

Is Your Child at Risk?

When you think of diabetes and children, type 1 diabetes probably first comes to mind. Once known as juvenile diabetes, type 1 affects mostly kids and young adults. But there's a new epidemic of type 2 diabetes popping up in youngsters. Type 2 was once so rare in young people that it was called adult-onset diabetes. Now, due in large part to the growing numbers of children who are overweight and inactive, type 2 is being diagnosed in kids as young as age 5, with minority children most at risk.

How can you protect your child? Adopt a healthier lifestyle as a family. Make sure that everyone keeps active for at least 30 minutes a day. Allow only an hour a day with the TV/VCR/computer. Stop buying soda, juice drinks, and junk food. Consider a blood-glucose test for any child who is overweight and sedentary and has a close family member with the disease, is a member of one of the ethnic minorities listed at right, or has a dark discoloration of the skin on the neck or skin folds, a symptom of insulin resistance that's most common in children.

How Did You Get Diabetes?

Your first reaction to a diagnosis of diabetes might be, "Why me?" If scientists knew the answer to that question, they might be able to prevent and cure the disease. Unfortunately, researchers aren't there yet. But there's much we do know about its causes. First, we know that type 2 diabetes is most common in African Americans, Native Americans, Pacific Islanders, Latinos, and some Asians. People belonging to these ethnic groups are up to twice as likely to develop this disease, suggesting there's a genetic component to diabetes. These people have genes that somehow make them more susceptible.

But genetics isn't the only factor in determining who gets diabetes. A lot has to do with your lifestyle—what you eat, how much you weigh, and how active you are, for example. In fact, it may be possible to prevent (or at least delay the development of) type 2 diabetes, even if it's in your genes, by staying fit and healthy, says Randy Horwitz, MD, medical director of the University of Arizona's Program in Integrative Medicine, who is genetically prone to diabetes himself.

There are several main risk factors that increase your odds of type 2 diabetes, if you are genetically susceptible.

Weight. An estimated 80 percent of people with type 2 diabetes are either overweight or obese. Extra pounds, especially around the waist, can cause insulin resistance, since fat cells have fewer insulin receptors than muscle cells.

Diet. People who eat a typical Western diet (including lots of refined carbohydrates and other processed foods) are at higher risk for type 2 diabetes. These foods are more likely to raise blood sugar levels, increase the workload of the pancreas, and add extra pounds.

Activity. Regular exercise lowers blood sugar levels, while being inactive raises them and can cause weight gain. In general, the more muscle you have, the more insulin receptors you have and the less insulin resistance.

DR. WEIL SAYS: "While it's true that heredity has a substantial influence on diabetes, genes alone can't explain our current epidemic. Since our genetic makeup hasn't changed dramatically in just 40 years, environmental factors like diet and exercise presumably account for the rapid rise in diabetes."

Diagnosis: The Moment of Truth

How did your doctor know that you have diabetes? Maybe early symptoms like feeling very tired or thirsty or urinating more often prompted a visit to your doctor. More likely, you had no symptoms, but your doctor discovered the condition by doing a routine blood sugar test. This test, called a fasting plasma glucose test, measures the amount of glucose in your blood after you've abstained from eating for at least eight hours. Or your doctor may have used other tests, like a random plasma glucose test (which doesn't require fasting) or an oral glucose tolerance test (OGTT), where your blood sugar is measured a few hours after drinking a solution of water and glucose.

According to the American Diabetes Association, everyone age 45 and older should have their blood sugar tested, especially if they're overweight or obese. If the test is normal, it should be repeated every three years. It's a good idea to get tested earlier and more frequently if you have a first-degree relative (parent or sibling) with diabetes, are a member of a high-risk ethnic group, have had gestational (pregnancy-associated) diabetes or given birth to a baby weighing more than 9 pounds, or have low HDL ("good") cholesterol or high triglyercides (blood fats), high blood pressure, or pre-diabetes (see page 12).

A diagnosis of diabetes means you have had a fasting plasma glucose value of 126 milligrams per deciliter, or a random plasma glucose level or OGTT of 200 mg/dl. Now, you'll need to have your blood sugar tested far more frequently than every three years. Your doctor will perform this and other tests much more often. In fact, you will have to start testing yourself regularly at home, which you'll read about in Chapter Two.

Not Quite Diabetes?

Diabetes isn't the only condition that can affect blood sugar. Other health problems, like metabolic syndrome, polycystic ovarian syndrome, and pre-diabetes, also involve insulin resistance. It's still unclear what causes these conditions, but, as with type 2 diabetes, a combination of genetic vulnerability and factors like being overweight and sedentary is likely responsible.

Unfortunately, many people with these common conditions aren't even aware they have them. That's a big problem, since all of them can greatly raise your risk of developing full-blown type 2 diabetes. But if you *know* you have metabolic syndrome, polycystic ovarian syndrome, or prediabetes,

Q&A

I have type 2 diabetes. Is my child at higher risk for the disease?

Yes. A tendency toward diabetes can be inherited: Your child has roughly a 1 in 13 chance of developing diabetes if you were diagnosed after age 50; that risk increases to 1 in 7 if you were diagnosed before age 50. Kids whose parents *both* have diabetes have about a 1 in 2 chance of getting the disease themselves.

But diabetes isn't inevitable, even for people with a strong family history. Genes alone aren't enough to cause diabetes; an inherited predisposition along with lifestyle factors like poor diet, inactivity, and extra weight increase your odds of getting diabetes. That's where prevention comes in. Experts estimate that some 90 percent of cases of type 2 diabetes could be avoided if people exercised more, ate better, and developed other healthy habits. In fact, the large Diabetes Prevention Program study found that people already diagnosed with prediabetes who followed a healthy diet, exercised 30 minutes five times a week, and lost just 5 to 7 percent of their body weight reduced their risk of diabetes by almost 60 percent (*New England Journal of Medicine*, February 7, 2002). You can help children ward off diabetes by serving wholesome foods, encouraging them to be physically active and maintain a healthy weight, and following the other measures discussed on page 10.

you can then take steps to prevent type 2 diabetes or delay its onset. These steps include the same lifestyle interventions—such as changes in diet and physical activity—that people with diabetes need to follow. If you have one of these conditions, much of the advice in this guide applies to you, too.

Prediabetes. Also known as impaired glucose tolerance and impaired fasting glucose, prediabetes is, as its name implies, a condition that often precedes diabetes. A diagnosis of prediabetes puts you at much higher risk of developing type 2 diabetes within the next 10 years. And even now, prediabetes puts you at risk for some of the health problems linked with the full-blown disease, like heart attack, stroke, memory loss, and some kinds of cancer. Prediabetes typically has no noticeable symptoms.

DIAGNOSED BY ▶ A fasting blood sugar test. Blood sugar levels that are higher than 100 mg/dl (normal), but lower than 126 mg/dl when fasting (full-blown diabetes), mean you have prediabetes.

TREATMENT ▶ Research shows that people at high risk for type 2 diabetes (including those with prediabetes) can lower their chances of developing the disease by almost 60 percent through a diet and exercise program such the one described in this guide. If necessary, your doctor may also prescribe an oral drug to help make your cells more sensitive to insulin.

A Brief History of Diabetes

Diabetes has been around since ancient times, but the ways it's diagnosed and treated have changed dramatically over the years. Here are some highlights in the evolution of diabetes care.

1500s BC
Diabetes is first described by ancient Egyptian healers who notice that ants are attracted to the sugary urine of people with a mysterious (and often deadly) disease that causes intense thirst and frequent urination.

250 BC
The term *diabetes* is coined. Its translation, "to go through," alludes to the observation that patients urinated often. Later, the word *mellitus*—Latin for honey—is added to reflect the connection to blood sugar and to distinguish it from diabetes insipidus, an endocrine disorder not involving insulin that's marked by increased production of nonsweet urine.

1000 AD
Greek physicians prescribe horseback riding to people with diabetes, which they believe will help ease frequent urination. During this time, practitioners diagnose the condition by tasting the urine, which is sweet in people with diabetes mellitus.

1798
Scientists learn that the sugar glucose is found in the blood, is higher in people with diabetes, and spills over into their urine.

1850s to 1920s
Various diabetes-specific diets are introduced, including those limited mainly to oatmeal, rice, potatoes, or milk. Other nutritional approaches include a high-sugar diet and near-starvation. Scientists mistakenly believed these diets would cure diabetes.

"Although I think the term prediabetes might sound unnecessarily alarmist, I know that early lifestyle interventions, such as changes in diet and physical activity, can prevent type 2 diabetes or delay its onset."

Metabolic syndrome. Also known as insulin resistance syndrome and syndrome X, this condition is actually a cluster of medical problems involving your cholesterol, blood pressure, and weight that are triggered by insulin resistance. Left untreated, metabolic syndrome can put you at high risk for type 2 diabetes and heart disease, and may also be responsible for up to half of all heart attacks.

DIAGNOSED BY ▶ There's no one test to identify metabolic syndrome. Instead, you must have a fasting blood glucose level of at least 100 mg/dl or oral glucose tolerance test (OGTT) score of 140 mg/dl or higher, plus high triglycerides (blood fats), low HDL ("good") cholesterol, high blood pressure, and excess weight around the waist.

TREATMENT ▶ Like prediabetes, metabolic syndrome can be nipped in the bud by weight loss and regular physical activity; the same oral drugs

---

1921 and 1922
Insulin is discovered and successfully used to treat humans.

1940s
Researchers determine a link between diabetes and eye disease.

1955
Oral drugs aimed at lowering blood sugar are developed.

1959
Scientists recognize that there are two main types of diabetes. Type 1 was then also called juvenile diabetes and insulin-dependent diabetes, since it was typically diagnosed in childhood and required regular insulin injections. Type 2 was also called adult-onset and non-insulin-dependent diabetes. Researchers also discover that a third type, gestational diabetes, occurs only during pregnancy but raises the risk of type 2 diabetes later in life.

1970s to 1980s
Blood glucose meters for home testing are created and perfected.

2002
The landmark Diabetes Prevention Program study shows that people at high risk for type 2 diabetes can dramatically lower their chances of developing the disease through diet and exercise, which are found to be more effective at this than an oral diabetes drug.

2003
A team of diabetes specialists establishes new diagnostic criteria for prediabetes, a condition preceding type 2 diabetes, and the number of Americans considered to have prediabetes increases by about 20 percent since the term was first coined in 2002.

2004
The World Health Organization announces the advent of a "devastating" diabetes epidemic, with the number of people with diabetes worldwide expected to more than double to 366 million by 2030.

used to treat diabetes can help improve insulin sensitivity in people with metabolic syndrome, although not as effectively as lifestyle measures.

Polycystic ovarian syndrome. Women with polycystic ovarian syndrome (PCOS) tend to be insulin resistant. High levels of insulin in the blood can trigger increased production of male sex hormones (women normally have small amounts). This hormonal imbalance can result in symptoms ranging from acne and excess body hair to infertility and multiple ovarian cysts. PCOS can also increase your risk of type 2 diabetes and heart disease.

DIAGNOSED BY ▶ Your doctor will order a number of blood tests, including a fasting blood glucose test or OGTT to check for insulin resistance and will also test your levels of various sex hormones.

TREATMENT ▶ As with other conditions involving insulin resistance, PCOS can be managed with weight control, a healthy diet, and regular exercise. Your physician may also prescribe birth control pills, which can help balance hormones, and perhaps an oral diabetes drug to increase insulin sensitivity.

CHAPTER TWO

Conventional Treatment

In Chapter One, you learned what diabetes is and what causes it. Now that you know more about this condition, you can work to keep it in check. But taking care of diabetes can feel like a full-time job, especially at first: There's a lot of information to absorb and skills to learn, from planning the right diet and making sure you get regular physical activity to learning how to test your own blood sugar on a regular basis and determining what medications you may need to take. To make this process feel less overwhelming, it's a good idea to get some health experts on your side. You can do this by choosing the practitioners that can best help you to control your diabetes and its potential side effects. These experts will work with you to keep your blood sugar levels in check through diet, exercise, and drugs, screen for possible complications like eye or foot problems, and help you cope with the emotional impact of having a chronic disease.

A lot of diabetes guides recommend that people with diabetes form a "health care team" to help them with these tasks. That's a little misleading. You'll definitely want some of the experts discussed here on your "team." But that doesn't mean you need to see all of these practitioners at once. More likely, you'll choose a few experts that you might see on a regular basis and add new ones when necessary, with some going to bat for you often and others mostly warming the bench. For example, you'll probably see your primary care physician or endocrinologist, a registered dietitian, and perhaps a diabetes educator most often. Some team players, like a podiatrist (foot doctor) and ophthalmologist (eye doctor), you'll only see once or twice a year. And you may add still others, such as a psychotherapist or exercise physi-

> "When you can't solve the problem, manage it."
>
> ROBERT H. SCHULLER

ologist, only if the need or interest arises. Whom you choose to see and how frequently you see them may also depend on your health insurance.

Choosing Team Players

Of all the experts you can choose for your team, you're probably most familiar with your primary care physician (PCP). A PCP is the doctor, usually either a family practitioner or internist, whom you visit regularly for general checkups or when you get sick. He is also probably the person who first diagnosed you with diabetes and who prescribes your diabetes medication. Or, your PCP may have recommended that you also see an endocrinologist, a doctor who has special training in treating diseases related to the endocrine (hormonal) system, like diabetes. If you don't choose to see an endocrinologist, it's a good idea to find a PCP who has experience treating a lot of patients with diabetes. In any case, you'll want to find a doctor who communicates well, listens to your concerns, and is open to new treatments, whether conventional or integrative. Not every physician is well-versed in all areas of integrative medicine—some may not know much about dietary supplements, for example—but many are open-minded when it comes to trying safe, natural measures. In truth, the very nature of diabetes treatment is integrative, says Program in Integrative Medicine medical director Randy Horwitz, MD, since it typically combines natural lifestyle measures like diet and exercise with conventional medications. Here's the lowdown on some of the other experts you may choose to see.

Certified diabetes educator. A certified diabetes educator (CDE) is a practitioner—usually a registered nurse, but sometimes a dietitian, social worker, or other health professional—who is specially trained to teach and care for people with diabetes. Seeing a CDE is like having a guide to help you learn the self-care skills you need and give you a pep talk when you feel less motivated. He or she can teach you how to buy and use a glucose meter to test your blood sugar, help you learn how to maximize the effectiveness of the medications you take, and plan for times like holidays or sick days when it may be more difficult to take care of yourself. If your CDE is also a dietitian, exercise physiologist, or therapist, she may be able to offer advice in these areas as well. Some CDEs teach diabetes-education classes to small groups of patients while others work one-on-one. They may do an initial consultation in person, and can provide follow-up support by phone or online. Ask your doctor for a referral, or see the Resource Guide on page 74 for more. Your health insurance company may also offer special diabetes-monitoring programs that provide education and support.

Registered dietitian. Trained in nutrition, a registered dietitian (RD) can help you plan meals, lose weight, and make healthy food choices. As you'll learn in Chapter Three, there's no one "diabetes diet" that's right for everyone with the disease, so an RD can work with you to put together an individual meal plan that's good for your blood sugar as well as your taste buds and culinary skills. An RD can also teach you concepts like dietary exchanges and carbohydrate counting (see page 24) and adapt diets to your specific needs, whether you're a vegetarian or have a coexisting medical concern like irritable bowel syndrome.

Eye doctor. Because diabetes can affect the blood vessels in your eyes, putting you at higher risk for sight-stealing conditions like glaucoma and retinopathy, you'll need to see an ophthalmologist or optometrist at least once a year to have your vision tested. Choose one who's familiar with diabetic eye disease.

Choosing a Glucose Meter

Let's face it: No one wants to have to stick themselves on a regular basis to test blood. But as recently as the early 1980s, blood glucose meters didn't even exist. Back then, people with diabetes had to rely on checking their urine with specialized test strips—less painful, but also far less accurate—to measure their blood sugar.

These days, scientists are working on developing new, pain-free ways to effectively monitor blood sugar. In the meantime, you have over 30 different options when it comes to glucose meters. Here are some things to consider when shopping for one (they're available at pharmacies, medical supply stores, and on the Internet, and are usually covered by health insurance). Ask your doctor or CDE for more recommendations.

Your physical limitations.
Do you have vision problems? Some glucose monitors have larger digital displays or even voice recordings that "talk" to you. Other meters offer the option of testing blood from your arm or thigh, which can be helpful for people with poor circulation to the fingers.

Size. Larger meters may be better for older eyes or shaky hands, while smaller machines can fit into a shirt pocket or purse.

Tech savvy. If you like gadgets, try a meter with computer compatibility, which will allow you to download results to special software that helps track your blood sugar over time.

The "ouch" factor. If you just can't get past the fear of pain or sight of blood, you do have a few options. The Personal Lasette Plus uses a laser to draw blood with less pain, although it's expensive. And the noninvasive GlucoWatch—a watchlike device you wear on your wrist—uses low-level electrical currents to test glucose without puncturing skin, but it's less accurate than traditional glucose meters and is meant to complement, not replace, them.

Cost. Your health insurer may only cover specific meters; check with your insurance provider before you buy one.

Podiatrist. A podiatrist is a specialist in treating foot problems. Since diabetes can cause problems with the nerves and blood vessels in your feet, you may be more prone to foot injuries and infections. You might not need to see a podiatrist on a regular basis unless you tend to have calluses, corns, bunions, or other complaints, but you and your PCP should check your feet regularly for signs of trouble (see page 58 for more).

Mental health professional. Living with diabetes can make you feel anxious, depressed, angry, stressed out, frustrated, or just plain overwhelmed. It may also affect how you get along with your friends, family, or coworkers. If this is true for you, you might want to consider seeing a psychologist, psychiatrist, social worker, or another trained mental health professional, who can help you cope with these and other concerns. (See Chapter Six for more.)

Exercise physiologist. Physical activity has many benefits for people with diabetes, from helping shed pounds to increasing insulin sensitivity. If you need help putting together an exercise plan that you can stick with, ask your doctor to recommend an exercise physiologist or another fitness professional to help.

DR. WEIL SAYS: "Although many people with type 2 diabetes and their doctors choose drug therapy because it seems easier than changes in lifestyle and behavior, regular activity and a healthier diet have the added benefit of reducing the risk for cardiovascular disease and other complications of diabetes."

Testing, Testing …

The one member of your health care "team" you'll see the most is your PCP (or endocrinologist). Before you were diagnosed with diabetes, you probably saw your doctor once a year for a checkup, or only when you got sick. Now, you'll need to visit your PCP several times a year or more, depending on how well you control your diabetes. During these visits, he'll check your body for complications and test your blood sugar. (You'll also start testing your blood sugar at home, as you'll read about next.) One of the most important blood tests your doctor can give you is the glycated hemoglobin test, called the A1C test for short. This test is helpful because it gives a picture of your average blood sugar over the past few months, not just the day you're tested.

To understand the value of the A1C, here's a quick science lesson: When you have diabetes, the extra sugar (glucose) in your blood attaches itself, or "glycates," to hemoglobin, the oxygen-carrying pigment in red blood cells. The more excess glucose in your blood, the more glycated hemoglobin as well. This is a permanent change—the hemoglobin stays glycated until the red blood cells naturally die. The A1C test measures the percentage of glycated hemoglobin in your blood. And because red blood cells live about 120 days, the A1C can show you this percentage over the past two or three months. That's important, since the A1C results can give you an idea of how your blood sugar levels change over time.

People without diabetes have an A1C score of about 5 percent ("normal"). If you have diabetes, though, your A1C will be higher. Most experts recommend that you aim for an A1C of less than 7 percent to minimize your risk of long-term diabetes complications. Diet, exercise, medications, and the other approaches discussed in this guide can help you keep your A1C under 7 percent. Your doctor will give you an A1C blood test every three to six months to see how well your treatment plan is working. You may also regularly be given other tests (for cholesterol, blood pressure, and more), as you'll read about in Chapter Eight.

Testing Blood Sugar at Home

Your doctor isn't the only one who needs to check your blood sugar. You also need to test it regularly at home. That way, you can tell how your diet and levels of stress and activity affect it, see how well medications are working, and help prevent diabetes complications. This is called self-monitoring of blood glucose (SMBG), and it means using a small, fine needle called a lancet to prick your skin (typically a finger, but sometimes your arm or thigh) and collect blood on a test strip, which is then "read" by a battery-operated machine called a blood glucose monitor. There's a wide variety of glucose monitors (see box on page 17), but all have the same goal of testing your blood sugar level, which will show up as a number on the monitor's digital screen. You'll keep a log of this number each time you test your blood sugar.

How often you check your blood sugar depends on where you are in your treatment plan. For example, if you've just been diagnosed with diabetes, your doctor may want you to practice SMBG several times a day. On the other hand, if you're following a diet and exercise program and are taking medication—and are seeing positive results—you may only need to

Q&A

Is there a cure for diabetes ?

Not yet. But you may be able to greatly control the condition with lifestyle measures and medications to the point where your blood sugar levels become "normal," putting the disease into remission. For example, if you were overweight when you were diagnosed with diabetes and then lost weight, your blood sugar would decrease. A program of regular physical activity can also greatly lower your blood sugar, even if you were previously inactive. However, that doesn't mean your diabetes has been "cured." If you gain back the weight you lost or stop exercising, your blood sugar levels will rise again, since the decreased production of insulin that occurs in people with diabetes can't be reversed. So it's important to keep following the measures mentioned in this book. While a healthy lifestyle can't completely eliminate diabetes, it *can* put the disease into remission and make it more manageable.

check your blood sugar a few times a week. In any case, you'll want your blood sugar levels to be as close to normal as possible. This means your test results should be in the range of 90 to 130 mg/dl for preprandial glucose (before you eat) and less than 180 mg/dl postprandial (one to two hours after a meal). Your doctor may set more specific SMBG goals for you.

The Lowdown on Diabetes Drugs

The first line of treatment for people with diabetes usually involves diet, weight loss, and exercise, says Victoria Rommel, MD, a family practitioner and University of Arizona Program in Integrative Medicine graduate Associate Fellow in Wadesboro, North Carolina, who treats many patients with type 2 diabetes. The other drug-free approaches discussed in this guide can also help. Sometimes, though, even your best efforts to keep blood sugar down naturally aren't enough. "In an ideal world, people with type 2 diabetes wouldn't need to take medication," says Dr. Rommel, "but it can be very helpful for some people." If your blood sugar levels remain high despite lifestyle measures, it may be time to ask your doctor about conventional treatment.

Say the word "diabetes" and insulin treatment probably first comes to mind. True, people with type 1 diabetes must rely on regular insulin injections simply to survive. But the same isn't necessarily true of people with type 2 diabetes. In fact, most of those with type 2 will never need to use insulin, because their bodies still produce it. And those who do, usually do not need it until they've had type 2 diabetes for many years.

Instead, your physician may prescribe one or more of the five main classes of oral diabetes drugs below. Each works in different ways to stabilize blood sugar, and none contains insulin. Which ones your doctor chooses may depend on your physical condition and their potential side effects, according to Duke endocrinologist Mark Feinglos, MD. For example, your physician may prescribe a biguanide (metformin) if you're also overweight, since this drug can aid weight loss, or an alpha-glucosidase inhibiting drug if your blood sugar typically spikes after eating. You'll need to take oral diabetes medications one to three times each day, and your doctor may prescribe more than one class of drug to control your blood sugar. Used in addition to (not instead of) a comprehensive lifestyle program for diabetes, oral diabetes drugs may stabilize your blood sugar enough to help you avoid using insulin injections in the future.

Sulfonylureas. The oldest class of oral diabetes drugs, sulfonylureas stimulate cells in the pancreas to release more insulin. Brand names include Diabeta, Glucotrol, and Micronase. Side effects range from nausea and weight gain to a hypoglycemic reaction (an episode of *too*-low blood sugar that makes you feel shaky, nervous, or lightheaded).

Biguanides. Currently, there's only one drug in this class, but it's quite popular. Glucophage (metformin) works by keeping your liver from releasing too much glucose. Side effects may include nausea and gas. Metformin may (rarely) cause a potentially fatal condition called lactic acidosis in people with liver or kidney problems, so it isn't recommended for them.

Meglitinides. Like sulfonylureas, these drugs (Prandin and Starlix) stimulate the pancreas to release more insulin and are usually taken at mealtime to prevent a rise in blood sugar after eating. They may cause headaches, diarrhea, and hypoglycemic reactions.

Thiazolidinediones. Called TZDs for short, these drugs (Actos and Avandia) help make your cells more sensitive to insulin. A third TZD, Rezulin, was taken off the market in 2000 after reports of some deaths due to liver damage. Even if you take one of the other two TZDs, you should have your liver enzymes tested regularly. Other side effects may include ankle swelling, weight gain, and muscle weakness.

Alpha-glucosidase inhibitors. Also known as "starch blockers," these drugs (Precose and Glyset) slow your body's digestion of starches, which break down into sugars. That makes the rise in blood sugar you typically experience after a meal slower and steadier than usual. Side effects include bloating, gas, and diarrhea, but these drugs don't promote weight gain, a plus for heavier people.

> **DR. WEIL SAYS:** "I'm concerned about the side effects—including possible liver toxicity—of oral diabetes drugs, and encourage patients to avoid or lower their dose of them by following lifestyle measures."

The Ins and Outs of Insulin

If you do need to take insulin injections, it doesn't mean that you've failed at controlling your diabetes. For some people, over time, even the best attempts to keep blood sugar low with lifestyle measures and oral medications may no longer be enough. Researchers suspect that's because the pancreas stops producing enough insulin, after all those years of trying to overcome insulin resistance. Such people need insulin injections to keep blood sugar levels in check and avoid diabetes-related complications.

A few people with type 2 diabetes may need to start off on a course of insulin injections right away: Those who are very overweight, don't get much physical activity, and have very high blood sugar may need to start using insulin as soon as they're diagnosed just to get their diabetes under control. Once they begin to lose weight and start exercising, and their blood sugar levels start to drop, they may be able to stop it.

If you have to take insulin, you'll likely need far less of it than people with type 1 diabetes, who must take injections several times a day. Most people with type 2 diabetes typically need only one or two insulin injections a day. There are many different kinds of insulin, either made synthetically in the lab or derived from animals. All types must be given as a shot, usually either with a syringe (needle) or a sharp, penlike device injected into the abdomen, where it's absorbed the quickest. If you need insulin, your doctor or CDE can tell you which kind you'll use and how to inject it. And remember, insulin, too, is an adjunct to, not a replacement for, a healthy lifestyle.

CHAPTER THREE

Healthy Eating for Diabetes

I f you're like many people, diet might seem to be the most confusing aspect of having diabetes. You might wonder what foods you can and can't eat or mistakenly believe that you need to avoid sugar completely. But it's completely possible to enjoy a diet that's both nutritious *and* tasty, says Jo-Anne Rizzotto, a registered dietitian and certified diabetes educator at Boston's Joslin Clinic. She points out that, with a few exceptions, people with diabetes generally need to follow the same basic guidelines for healthy nutrition as everyone else. In fact, following a healthy diet can help you get your diabetes under control and lower your risk of developing complications, as you'll read in this chapter.

> "Food is our common ground, a universal experience."
>
> JAMES BEARD

How Food Affects Blood Sugar

What you eat can affect your stomach and your taste buds. But food can also influence your blood sugar levels: Eating certain foods or too much of them can make your blood sugar temporarily surge, whether or not you have diabetes. Lots of people mistakenly believe that only foods high in sugar like cookies, cakes, and candies have this effect. But your blood sugar can rise when you eat *any* foods rich in carbohydrates ("carbs"), including not just sweets but also fruit, milk, bread, pasta, and starchy vegetables like corn and potatoes. Your body breaks down the carbs in these foods into glucose. Some foods contain more carbs and will therefore produce more glucose. Foods that also contain fat or protein are digested more slowly and don't increase blood sugar as quickly as those that are mostly pure carbohydrate. For example, a piece of bread dipped in a bit of olive oil will raise your blood

Q&A

I've noticed drinks, snack bars, and other foods aimed at people with diabetes. Should I try them?

Glucerna, Choice DM, Extend, and other brands of diabetic bars and beverages typically contain a mix of fiber, fat, protein, carbohydrates, and certain vitamins and minerals meant to help improve blood sugar and lower the risk of heart disease and other diabetes-related complications. These products *can* have a place in a balanced diet for people with diabetes, but you need to decide how best to fit them in, says dietitian Jo-Anne Rizzotto. For example, a snack bar with 100 calories, about 60 percent of which come from carbohydrates, would make a good snack before exercising, since it may help prevent hypoglycemia. On the other hand, a shake that contains twice as many calories and is fortified with vitamins and minerals is better used as a total meal replacement for occasions when you don't have time to eat. In any case, these products shouldn't be used to routinely replace other healthy foods, and you'll need to read their labels carefully and work with your dietitian to determine how to fit them into a balanced diet plan.

sugar more slowly than if you ate the bread alone. It's fine to eat carb-rich foods in moderation if you have diabetes, but if you eat a lot of them consistently, your blood sugar can remain high. That's why people with diabetes need to keep track of both the amount and the type of carbs they eat.

Just as eating a diet high in carbs can keep blood sugar levels high, sticking to a meal plan that's high in fiber, whole grains, beans, produce, nuts, fish, and other healthy foods has been shown to help control blood sugar. Plus, one study found that good eating habits—like limiting high-sugar and high-fat foods, eating lots of vegetables, and planning meals in advance—are at least as important as diabetes medications for controlling blood sugar (*Journal of the American Dietetic Association*, April 2004).

DR. WEIL SAYS: "Although sugar was once taboo for people with diabetes, we now know that white flour, corn sweeteners, and other highly refined carbohydrates cause even greater spikes in blood sugar levels. You should eat these foods only in limited amounts."

Getting Started: See Your RD

While the general nutrition guidelines you'll read about here are a great way to learn the basics of eating for diabetes, there's no one diet that's right for everyone with this disease. Your individual dietary needs may differ depending on whether you need to lose weight, have heart or kidney disease, or use insulin, for example. That's why it's important to visit a registered dietitian (RD), preferably one who's a certified diabetes educator, for advice on putting together the best meal plan for you. Ideally, you should see a dietitian when you're first diagnosed with diabetes and then at least every six months to a year. She'll help you determine how many calories you need based on your age, gender, weight, and activity level; teach you how to eat healthier for good blood sugar control; and help you adapt your meal plan for special occasions or any other concerns you have. Here are three meal-planning approaches the two of you may discuss.

Carbohydrate counting. This meal-planning approach allows you to track the carbohydrates you eat throughout the day. It's based on the idea that, since all carbs raise blood sugar, focusing on how much carbohydrate you eat at each meal and snack can help control diabetes. This approach also allows people with diabetes more flexibility in their food choices, says

Try This: Planning for Special Occasions

Having diabetes doesn't have to put a damper on dining out, holiday gatherings, or other food-oriented celebrations. By using the same advance planning you would to lose weight or monitor your carb consumption, you can enjoy yourself without feeling guilty. Next time you're faced with a dinner out or a holiday party, try these tips from Jo-Anne Rizzotto, RD, and others.

- Don't go to special functions overly hungry. Some people with diabetes think that if they don't eat all day, they can indulge later, but this just causes them to overeat. Instead, eat a healthy snack beforehand, and then enjoy—but don't stuff—yourself at the party.

- Plan ahead to balance carbohydrates. When you're at an Italian restaurant, for example, consider skipping or eating a smaller portion of pasta if you're also having bread with your meal.

- If you want to have dessert, eat a filling appetizer or a salad as your meal.

- Practice mindful eating: Eat slowly, savor the experience, and take pleasure in the company of your dining companions. You'll likely eat less but enjoy it more if you slow down the pace of your meal.

- Don't beat yourself up. If you eat healthfully most of the time, you shouldn't feel guilty if you occasionally go off your meal plan on special occasions.

Jo-Anne Rizzotto. When you're carb counting, your RD will first calculate the number of grams of carbohydrates you should eat each day, based on your age, size, calorie needs, activity level, what you like to eat, and whether or not you need to lose weight. Exceeding this number may cause your blood sugar to rise, while not getting enough carbs may mean your blood sugar drops too low. Then you decide how to use these grams throughout the day. If you're an older man or a woman who needs to shed some extra pounds, your allotted number of daily carb grams might be 160. Now you'll count the carb grams in each food you eat, using a nutrition book, "carb counter" list (available at supermarkets and online), or by reading food labels. Although you can "spend" that 160 grams any way you like, it's important to remember that some choices are still better than others: A banana and a candy bar both contain about 30 grams of carbs, for example, but the banana has more nutrients and far less fat and fewer calories than the candy, making it a more nutritious choice.

Diabetic exchanges. Some people with diabetes use exchanges—groupings of foods that are similar nutritionally—to plan their meals. With exchanges, foods have been placed into categories based on their similar composition of carbohydrates, fat, protein, and calories. The seven exchange groups are starches, milk, fruit, vegetables, meats (and meat substitutes), fats, and sweets. Your RD can help determine how many exchanges

Meatless Eating with Diabetes

If you have diabetes and want to be a vegetarian, there's good news: It's possible to consume a healthy plant-based diet and manage your condition successfully. In fact, meatless eating can *benefit* diabetes because such a diet typically contains more dietary fiber, which helps control blood sugar levels. Reducing the amount of animal products in your diet can help lower your fat and cholesterol intake, decreasing the risk for heart disease. (You can get enough protein by eating beans, peas, lentils, soy foods, whole grains, nuts, and seeds; some so-called vegetarians also eat dairy products, eggs, and even chicken or fish.) In addition, you may take in fewer calories and lose some weight, which can make a difference in controlling type 2 diabetes. Meanwhile, one small, preliminary study of people with type 2 diabetes who were placed on a strict vegan diet (containing no animal products) for three months found that it reduced their fasting blood sugar by an average of 28 percent, and many patients needed less medication. For more, speak with your RD, who can offer advice on how people with diabetes can follow a vegetarian diet, and check out a cookbook such as *Month of Meals: Vegetarian Pleasures* from the American Diabetes Association.

you should eat at each meal. For instance, you might be allowed two starch exchanges at lunch (in addition to vegetable, fruit, fat, milk, and meat exchanges). Your RD will give you an exchange list, which notes the types of foods in each category and common serving sizes. Looking at that list, you might see that you could have one slice of bread and 1/3 cup of brown rice as your lunchtime starches. Exchanges can be useful, but Rizzotto says she prefers to use carb counting with her clients, since most people find it an easier concept to understand.

Glycemic index. Although all carbs raise blood sugar, it's also true that some of them raise it faster than others. To help you choose the ones that won't spike blood sugar too quickly, your RD may teach you about the glycemic index (GI), which measures how easily the body turns a particular food into glucose. The GI rates foods on a scale of 0 to 100, with a rating of over 70 considered high, and a rating under 55 low. The higher the GI score of a food, the faster the body will convert it to glucose. Foods like white rice, corn flakes, and white bread rank high on the GI, while whole grains, beans, and most vegetables are low. Of course, not all low-GI foods are nutritious—ice cream and some candy bars, for example, are high in calories and unhealthy fats—so consider a food's complete nutrient profile when choosing from the GI.

Some RDs question the rating of foods on the GI and doubt its usefulness, but Rizzotto and a growing number of others believe it can be a helpful educational tool for controlling diabetes. You don't need to memorize the entire GI (which includes over 600 foods), but you should get a basic idea of what foods are high and low. For more information, see *www.glycemicindex.com*.

Eating Well with Diabetes

In general, about 45 to 50 percent of your daily calories should come from carbohydrates. But eating for diabetes isn't just about focusing on carbs. Other foods and compounds can be good (and not so good) for you. Here are some additional things to consider when planning your meals.

Sugar. The idea that people with diabetes can't eat sugar is one of the biggest misconceptions about the disease, says Jo-Anne Rizzotto. In fact, many patients actually avoid sweets but still eat a lot of other refined carbs (like white bread and white rice), which are just as bad for blood sugar levels, adds Program in Integrative Medicine medical director Randy Horwitz,

MD. When it comes to carbs, you need to strike a balance. It's okay to indulge in the occasional cookie or piece of candy, but you should eat it instead of, not in addition to, other carbs. Keep in mind that when you see the words sucrose (table sugar), fructose (fruit sugar), maple syrup, molasses, corn syrup, and honey on a food label, they all count as "sugar" as far as diabetes is concerned.

As for alternative sweeteners, aspartame (NutraSweet), saccharin, sucralose (Splenda), and the herb stevia (available in health food stores) are all safe for people with diabetes to consume. But that doesn't mean you can eat more of the foods that contain them: Foods marked "sugar-free" may still contain other refined carbs and unhealthy fats, so you'll need to read ingredients labels carefully.

> **DR. WEIL SAYS:** "I encourage people to become familiar with the newer method of evaluating carbs by paying attention to the glycemic index."

Fat. Most experts recommend that people with diabetes get between 25 to 30 percent of their daily calories from fat, with less than 10 percent of those calories coming from saturated fat (in meat, milk, butter, cheese, and other animal products). You should also eliminate trans fatty acids from your diet. These fats, found in margarine and many fried and processed foods, can raise cholesterol, increasing your risk of heart disease. Replace saturated and trans fats with monounsaturated fats (found in olive and canola oils, nuts, and seeds), which have been shown in some studies to lower blood sugar and triglycerides (blood fats). The omega-3 fatty acids in salmon, sardines, flaxseed, and walnuts also have heart-protective qualities in people with diabetes; eat a few servings of them a week.

Protein. People with diabetes should generally get the same amount of protein—about 15 to 20 percent of daily calories—as people without this disease. Fish, as well as plant-based proteins like soy and other beans, tend to be healthier choices than meat because they're also lower in saturated fat. If you have kidney disease, check with your RD, who will likely advise you to follow a lower-protein diet (excess protein can strain the kidneys).

Fiber. Research shows that people who eat diets low in fiber have more than twice the risk of developing diabetes as those who consume more. Even if you already have diabetes, studies suggest that a very-high-fiber diet (50 grams a day) can reduce blood sugar, cholesterol, and triglycerides. Two

Q&A

I've heard that cinnamon is good for people with diabetes. Is this true?

Yes, there's some preliminary evidence that cinnamon may help reduce blood sugar. In one study, 60 people with type 2 diabetes were given either daily capsules with 1, 3, or 6 grams of cinnamon (one gram equals one-half teaspoon) or placebos for 40 days. Compared to people who did not receive the spice, those who took cinnamon supplements in any amount not only dropped their blood sugar levels by some 18 to 29 percent, but they also had reductions in LDL ("bad") and total cholesterol as well as triglycerides (*Diabetes Care*, December 2003). Scientists believe cinnamon may contain compounds that make cells more responsive to insulin. For now, these promising findings come from just one small human study (as well as from lab and animal research), and cinnamon was given to people in capsule form, which isn't widely available as a supplement. Although more research is needed, it's safe and reasonable to experiment by adding one-quarter teaspoon of cinnamon twice a day to cereal, salads, toast, or juice and other beverages. (It's low in carbohydrates and calories.) But don't use this spice in place of oral diabetes medications or insulin or substitute it for the other lifestyle measures recommended in this book.

fiber-rich foods are discussed in detail below. Other good sources of fiber include fruits, vegetables, and beans. Plus, a daily supplement such as psyllium (in Metamucil) can help you get enough fiber and lower cholesterol.

Whole grains. Numerous studies have shown that eating plenty of whole grains like brown rice, dark breads, wheat germ, and bran and other cereals significantly reduces the risk of diabetes. Researchers suspect that the fiber, magnesium, and other beneficial compounds in whole grains may be responsible. Although more research needs to be done in people who already have diabetes, it's a good idea to aim for several servings of whole grains a day.

Nuts. Research also suggests that people who eat at least five one-ounce servings of nuts or nut butter a week have a lower risk of diabetes, possibly because of the fiber, magnesium, and monounsaturated fats they contain. Because nuts have been shown to lower blood sugar and reduce the risk of heart problems, it's reasonable for people with diabetes to snack on them, but you should eat them instead of, not in addition to, other high-fat or high-calorie foods.

Alcohol. In some studies, one-half to two glasses of alcohol a day have been shown to reduce the risk of diabetes as well as protect against heart disease in people who already have diabetes. Yet, alcohol can trigger hypoglycemia in people who use insulin or take oral sulfonylurea diabetes drugs. This can be a problem, since the symptoms of hypoglycemia can be confused with those of being intoxicated, making it difficult for you and people around you to know whether you're having a diabetic emergency or are a little tipsy. To be on the safe side, discuss alcohol with your doctor or RD before choosing to imbibe.

Caffeine. Drinking a lot of coffee might help prevent diabetes, according to some research. In a recent study, people who drank at least 10 cups of coffee daily had up to a 79 percent lower risk of developing the disease, compared to those who drank two or fewer daily cups (*Journal of the American Medical Association*, March 10, 2004). Researchers aren't sure how coffee helps or whether its benefits have to do with the caffeine it contains. But other studies suggest that caffeine can be a problem for people with diabetes by actually raising blood sugar and reducing blood flow to the brain, mimicking a hypoglycemic reaction. A daily cup or two of coffee or other caffeinated beverages should be fine, says Jo-Anne Rizzotto, but too much caffeine can dehydrate you, so check with an RD if you're concerned.

CHAPTER FOUR

Staying Fit with Diabetes

ietary changes and conventional approaches like medication and insulin are probably the best-known treatments for diabetes. But exercise is equally important in managing your blood sugar levels. In fact, you should look at getting physical activity just as you would taking oral diabetes medication or giving yourself a shot of insulin, says Kirsten Ward, an exercise physiologist at Boston's Joslin Clinic. She points out that, like taking medication and following a healthy diet, exercise is something you need to do regularly to help control your diabetes. That may seem easier said than done, especially if—like many people with type 2 diabetes—you're currently a bit of a couch potato. But physical activity doesn't have to be a chore or something you dread: You can make movement an enjoyable part of your diabetes treatment program by following the tips in this chapter.

Why Movement Matters

Regular exercise has long been recognized as a useful treatment for diabetes. As far back as 600 AD, Chinese physicians recommended that people with diabetes walk more than 120 steps before each meal to ease this condition. These days, science has caught up to such recommendations, with numerous studies showing a direct link between physical activity and good blood sugar control. Some research has found that people who get more physical activity are at decreased risk for developing diabetes in the first place, while other studies show that people who already have this condition can increase insulin sensitivity—and sometimes eliminate or lower

> "Every man is the builder of a temple called his body."
>
> HENRY DAVID THOREAU

their dose of diabetes medication—by exercising regularly.

Physical activity can improve diabetes in a number of different ways. First, after about 15 minutes of exercise, your body begins to use the glucose stored in your muscles and liver for fuel. Beyond that point, as you keep moving, your body turns to the glucose in your blood, which helps to bring down blood sugar. Activity can also make your muscles and other tissues more sensitive to insulin, meaning that your body needs less of this hormone to move glucose into cells where it's needed for fuel. Plus, exercise helps control weight and ease stress (two factors that can elevate blood sugar) and can reduce the risk of diabetes-related complications like cardiovascular disease. Perhaps most impressive, research shows that a single session of moderate-intensity activity can increase insulin sensitivity and lower blood sugar for up to a day or so afterward. That's important, since it means that (with your doctor's supervision) you may be able to discontinue or decrease your dose of oral diabetes drugs or insulin by exercising on a regular basis.

Try This: Shopping for Shoes

When it comes to some types of physical activity—especially walking—the only "equipment" you need is a good pair of athletic shoes. That's even more important when you have a form of diabetes-related nerve damage called peripheral neuropathy (PN), which can affect sensation in your feet. If your feet are numb, you may not be able to feel whether your shoes are too tight. Left untreated, blisters, abrasions, and other small injuries from ill-fitting shoes can become infected. But you can help prevent such problems by buying exercise footwear that fits you properly. Here are some shopping tips for doing just that:

• Have your feet measured each time you buy new shoes, since feet tend to get bigger with age. Keep in mind that your feet may be two different sizes, and that the sizing and fit of shoes can vary from manufacturer to manufacturer.

• Buy shoes at the end of the day, when your feet (which can swell) are their largest.

• There should be a small space between the end of your longest toe and the end of the shoe to ensure that your shoes aren't too small and that your toes don't rub against the end of the shoe.

• Choose synthetic-fiber socks that wick away perspiration, and wear them when trying on shoes. Some medical supply and diabetes supply stores and websites sell socks for people with diabetes that have special cushioning and no seams (which can irritate feet).

• Walk around in the shoes to make sure they're comfortable and try to replicate some of the motions your foot might make in them, such as running or walking uphill. Remember, you shouldn't need to "break in" new shoes: If they don't fit, don't buy them.

Getting Started, Safely

It's clear that exercise can be a boon to people with diabetes. But before you get moving, it's a good idea to take a few precautions. First, Kirsten Ward advises everyone with diabetes to get a physician's approval before starting a workout program. This is especially important if you also have diabetes complications: If you have cardiovascular disease, for example, you may be asked to take a treadmill stress test to ensure that your heart can handle moderate exercise. And if you have diabetic retinopathy, you may need to avoid high-impact, high-intensity activities like weight lifting, sprinting, running, and scuba diving, which can increase blood pressure, worsening this condition. For the most part, though, almost everyone with diabetes can find some type of exercise they can safely enjoy. For instance, if neuropathy in your feet makes walking difficult, try water aerobics or swimming instead, suggests Program in Integrative Medicine medical director Randy Horwitz, MD.

No matter what type of activities you choose, Ward advises checking your blood sugar about five minutes before and after exercising (if you're planning a long or strenuous workout, she recommends checking glucose during the activity as well). Drink plenty of water while working out, and consider eating a small carbohydrate-rich snack such as a piece of fruit or some crackers before exercising if your sugar is too low. If you find that physical activity significantly lowers your blood sugar, she says, talk with your doctor about the possibility of lowering your dose of oral diabetes drugs or insulin.

Your Exercise Prescription

Physical activity's blood-sugar-lowering benefits are similar to those of a drug, and they also only last a day or two. That's why it's important to exercise often: As with medications or insulin, you need regular "doses" of activity to maintain these positive results, says Mark Feinglos, MD, chief of endocrinology at Duke University Medical Center. In fact, some physicians are now writing their exercise recommendations on prescription pads to show patients just how important activity is. Once you begin viewing exercise as a vital part of your diabetes treatment, you may be more apt to start—and stick with—a regular program. Remember, it's fine to start slowly, adding time and varying your activities as you get used to breaking a sweat. Be sure to begin and end each workout with a 5- to 10-minute warm-up and cool-down such as slow walking. A personal trainer, exercise physiologist, or other fitness professional can also help you put together a workout program that's both effective and enjoyable and incorporates the following three elements.

Aerobic activity. Any movement that gets your heart pumping and makes you breathe harder is considered aerobic exercise. But you don't need to run or do jumping jacks—unless you want to, of course. There are many other aerobic options to choose from, including brisk walking; cycling (on an exercise bicycle at home or the gym, or on a real bike outdoors); swimming and water aerobics (good for people with neuropathy in their feet or who have arthritis or are overweight); dancing; hiking; using fitness equipment like elliptical trainers, stair steppers, and rowing machines; and more. Lighter activities like gardening, housework, and golf may not significantly lower cardiovascular risk, but they should still help reduce blood sugar, says Kirsten Ward.

WHY YOU NEED IT ▶ Aerobic activities are currently the best-studied form of exercise when it comes to diabetes control, and also have the most proven benefits for your heart and weight loss. If you're newly active, Ward suggests starting with aerobic exercise and adding strength training and flexibility activities after you've made a consistent aerobic program a habit.

RECOMMENDED DOSE ▶ The American College of Sports Medicine suggests that people with diabetes get between 20 and 60 minutes of aerobic activity a day, three to five days a week (work up to the high end of this recommendation if your goal is to lose or maintain weight). Start with 5 to 10 minutes a day if necessary, gradually increasing your duration over time.

Strength training. Also known as resistance training, this form of activity helps preserve bone, firm muscle, and shed pounds. It typically involves lifting "free" weights (dumbbells) or using weight machines (such as Nautilus), but you can also tone up with resistance tubing (sold at sporting goods stores), large rubber exercise bands, or the natural resistance of water or

Try This: Using a Pedometer

Looking for a fun way to keep moving? Try a pedometer. These small electronic gadgets clip onto your belt and count the number of steps that you take. Exercise physiologist Kirsten Ward says that a pedometer can be a great motivational tool to learn how much exercise you get each day. Although the target for most people is about 10,000 steps a day, you can use a pedometer to set individual goals—adding, say, 100 more steps a day if you currently get less. Pedometers can be a step in the right direction for those with diabetes: Some research has found that people with diabetes who use pedometers are more motivated to exercise than those who do not. You can find pedometers, often for $20 or less, at department stores and sporting goods stores.

your own body (like pushups and sit-ups).

WHY YOU NEED IT ▶ Although more studies show a correlation between aerobic exercise and reduced blood sugar levels, some research suggests that when strength training is done regularly, it can also increase insulin sensitivity, as well as improve symptoms of peripheral neuropathy (nerve damage) in people with diabetes.

RECOMMENDED DOSE ▶ According to experts, most people with diabetes should plan to do strength-training exercises about two or three days a week; aim for at least one set (8 to 15 repetitions) each of exercises that work the major muscle groups, like your arms, legs, abdominals, buttocks, and back. If you're using weights, ask a fitness professional to show you proper form and help you determine the correct number of pounds to lift; light weights may be best, especially at first. *Note:* People who also have diabetic retinopathy (see Chapter Eight), uncontrolled hypertension, or similar diabetes complications should avoid lifting heavy weights, since this can spike blood pressure.

Flexibility exercise. Whether it's yoga, Pilates, tai chi, qigong, or any one of a number of different types of flexibility exercises, regularly stretching your muscles and joints can improve your overall fitness.

WHY YOU NEED IT ▶ Flexibility exercises that stretch your muscles are an integral part of any fitness program because they increase your joints' range of motion and may help prevent injuries. For people with diabetes, they help minimize glycosylation, a problem in which high blood sugar levels can reduce joint flexibility. What's more, adding activities like yoga, Pilates, or the martial arts can spice up your exercise program, prevent boredom, and provide an outlet to ease stress.

RECOMMENDED DOSE ▶ Experts recommend that people with diabetes get at least 10 minutes of stretching or other flexibility exercises two or three days each week.

DR. WEIL SAYS: "Ideally exercise should be fun, not drudgery. Young children will wrestle playfully for hours, developing strength, coordination, and agility while getting a terrific aerobic workout and having the time of their lives. It's a pity that more grownups don't do the same."

Making Exercise a Part of Your Life

If you've been inactive until now, the exercise recommendations you just read may seem overwhelming. True, it can be very difficult to start getting regular physical activity when a short walk around the block leaves you winded and wiped out right now. Or, you may simply feel like you don't have enough time during your day to fit in a workout, or that exercise is boring or a chore.

These are all common roadblocks that you may encounter on the journey to better diabetes control, and ones that Kirsten Ward and other experts have lots of experience dealing with. Fortunately, they've brainstormed lots of great ideas to help you make physical activity a habit, and an enjoyable one at that. First, identify your weaknesses and excuses for not exercising, like those mentioned above. Then, choose some tactics from the list here to help get—and keep—you moving.

Change your thinking. "When we were kids, most of us looked forward to recess and getting outside to play," Ward points out. "But now adults see physical activity as a chore. It's time to start viewing it as recreation again." By thinking of exercise as playtime rather than work, you may find yourself looking forward to and not avoiding it.

Learn what you like. Before you can expect to commit to a regular workout routine, you need to figure out what types of activities you might find fun. Are you a social butterfly? Maybe you're better suited to exercising with others at a health club or in a class, or playing team sports like doubles tennis or softball. Is shopping your passion? Plan to walk brisk laps at the local mall for a half-hour before hitting the stores, suggests Dr. Feinglos.

Schedule workout times. You wouldn't blow off an important meeting at work, so why not treat physical activity the same way? Make exercise a priority by scheduling it on your calendar. If you tend to talk yourself out of exercise, set aside five blocks of time for workouts, advises Kirsten Ward. Even if you only fulfill three of those commitments, it's better than scheduling three appointments and not sticking to any of them.

Get others involved. Recruiting an exercise buddy can help, because you're more likely to stick with your routine if you're accountable to someone else. If finances allow, consider a personal trainer, who can also keep you motivated and on track. It's also a great idea to include your family in an exercise program: You'll not only set a good example for your kids or grandchildren, but you'll encourage your loved ones to get in shape, too.

Move more. You can become more active in general by making small changes in your life: Take the stairs—even just one flight to start—instead of the elevator. Park your car farther from store entrances rather than waiting for the closest parking space. Deliver messages to coworkers in person rather than via email. And seek out hobbies that involve physical activity, even if it's mild intensity, such as gardening or bird watching.

Make an investment. If you're a homebody who finds the prospect of using a gym membership or taking a daily walk in the park unlikely, consider investing in a piece of home exercise equipment (like a treadmill or exercise bike) if you can afford it. Dr. Horwitz suggests this tip, which he uses with his children: Park an exercise bike in front of your television set and view the equipment as a generator—you can't watch TV unless you ride the bike at the same time.

CHAPTER FIVE

Controlling Your Weight

f you've got diabetes and have been told to slim down, you've got company: More than 80 percent of people with diabetes are either overweight or obese. Researchers still aren't sure exactly how weight affects blood sugar, but there's some evidence that fat cells produce hormones and other substances that trigger insulin resistance. In addition, studies suggest that people with "apple"-shaped bodies, who carry weight around their waists, are more likely to have diabetes than those who are "pear"-shaped and gain weight mostly in the hips. This extra fat around the abdomen (known as visceral fat) somehow promotes insulin resistance.

But extra pounds alone aren't enough to cause diabetes, since it's quite possible to be obese but not have problems with insulin resistance, or even to be slim but still have type 2 diabetes. Instead, experts suspect that some people are born with a genetic predisposition to diabetes, which can trigger the disease when they gain too much weight. Yet, as you'll learn in this chapter, even people who already have the disease can lower their blood sugar by taking off some pounds.

> "My doctor told me to stop having intimate dinners for four—unless there are three other people."
>
> ORSON WELLES

Lessons from the Pimas

To get an idea of how weight affects the risk of diabetes, it's worth taking a look at the Pima Indians. This Arizona tribe—and their close relatives in Mexico—has been studied for the past several decades because of the effect that lifestyle factors like diet and inactivity have had on their blood sugar.

For millennia, the Mexican Pimas have grown their own food (typically lower-glycemic fare like wheat, beans, corn, and squash) and are also very physically active. Because they live in a harsh environment, they have endured times of famine and are quite lean, with very low rates of diabetes. Researchers say the Pimas possess "thrifty" genes, which allow them to store body fat in times of plenty so they don't starve during times of famine.

Some of these Pimas migrated to southern Arizona, where they lived similarly to their Mexican relatives. But by the turn of the 20th century, the water supply of the Arizona Pimas had been diverted by white settlers, and they began eating foods made with government surplus supplies like lard, sugar, and white flour. Without their farms to oversee, they also became more sedentary. The Arizona Pimas still had their thrifty genes, but famines became a rarity. As a result, the Arizona Pimas began gaining weight. Today most of them are obese, and more than half of them have been diagnosed with type 2 diabetes. But the Mexican Pimas, who have retained their healthy way of life, are nearly free of the disease, even though they share the same genes. Clearly, lifestyle influences your risk of diabetes.

Picking and Choosing Portions

When you're trying to eat healthy and lose weight, you'll need to pay attention to the portion sizes of your food, which take into account both *what* you eat and drink and *how much*. Actually, if you're like most people, you've been over-estimating the amount of food that makes up a true portion. Once you've got a good idea of the amount you're eating and drinking, however, you'll find it easier to make a conscious effort to reduce your portion sizes.

A portion is the actual amount of food that's right for you—for your age, gender, activity level, and health needs. On the other hand, a serving is simply a unit of measure. For example, a "serving" recommended by the Food Guide Pyramid may seem skimpy when you realize that one-half cup of cooked pasta is one bread serving, and it's easy to get six bread servings with just a restaurant plate of pasta. Also, know that a serving on a food label is for comparison shopping and may *not* be the same as a Pyramid serving.

First, figure out which foods or beverages supply you with the most calories. Common culprits are starchy, fatty, and sugary foods. Next, weigh and measure some common serving sizes. Then place a reasonable portion on your plate or in your bowl. You'll also want to find out how much liquid your glassware and mugs can hold, and identify a four- and eight-ounce serving. Try to form a mental snapshot of these quantities.

A quick way to gauge an appropriate portion of meat or fish is to compare it to the size of your palm or a deck of cards. For starchy side dishes or a medium fruit, your portion should be about the size of a tennis ball, while one ounce of cheese is comparable to four dice.

One way to evaluate your portions is by looking at how much space they take up on your plate. The goal is for plant-based foods to displace other, higher-calorie foods on your plate, such as animal sources of protein. Ideally, vegetables should take up at least half of your dinner plate, while grains and a protein source (such as fish, soy foods, beans, or poultry) equally make up the remaining half. Another way to eat smaller portions and not feel deprived is to use a salad plate rather than a dinner plate.

"When humans were living near starvation or had a feast-or-famine kind of eating, it was an advantage to have type 2 diabetes because it allowed you to store fat. Now, with food available all the time, those genes work against us. Perhaps diabetes is not a disease in itself but rather an alternative genetic constitution that becomes a disease only in relationship to lifestyle and environment."

How Weight Loss Helps

As the Pima Indians illustrate, it's possible to have genes that make you prone to diabetes without developing the disease itself as long as you avoid triggers like weight gain. That's best accomplished with a combination of lifestyle approaches like eating a healthy diet and regular physical activity. Of course, that might seem easier said than done, especially if you're significantly overweight. The good news? Research has shown that losing even small amounts of weight can lower the risk of full-blown diabetes in people who have already been diagnosed with prediabetes. In fact, in the large Diabetes Prevention Program study, people with prediabetes who lost just 7 percent of their body weight (an average of 10 to 15 pounds) through diet and exercise reduced their risk of diabetes by 58 percent—compared to just a 31 percent risk reduction in those who simply took the oral diabetes drug metformin (*New England Journal of Medicine*, February 7, 2002).

Other research suggests that people who already have diabetes can greatly benefit from moderate weight loss as well. Losing just 2.5 percent of your total weight can reduce your risk of cardiovascular disease, a worrisome complication of diabetes. And there's evidence that shedding even more pounds (10 to 15 percent of total body weight) can help stabilize blood sugar levels enough to allow some patients to discontinue their oral diabetes medications. Interestingly, one study has found that even people with diabetes who try but *fail* to lose weight appear to live longer than those don't attempt to shed pounds at all, possibly because people trying to slim down are more likely to eat healthy foods, exercise, and not smoke (*Diabetes Care*, March 2004). With results like these, there's no time like the present to give weight loss a shot.

Q&A

Will weight–loss surgery or liposuction improve my diabetes?

Although these surgical methods can help you slim down, the evidence is mixed when it comes to their effect on blood sugar levels: In one study, 64 percent of people with diabetes had a remission of the disease within one year of undergoing gastric bypass ("stomach stapling") surgery, while an additional 26 percent of patients saw improvements in their diabetes control (*Diabetes Care*, February 2002). Meanwhile, other research has found that liposuction (surgical fat removal) has no effect on insulin sensitivity or heart disease risk factors (*New England Journal of Medicine*, June 17, 2004). Researchers speculate that gastric bypass may be the more effective of the two because, like dieting, it helps shrink all the body's fat cells rather than simply removing them from certain areas. In any case, these procedures are serious measures that you should only undergo after discussing their potential risks and benefits with your physician.

Losing Weight Sensibly

A weight loss plan for someone who has diabetes isn't all that different from a diet for someone without the disease, according to Jo-Anne Rizzotto, a registered dietitian (RD) and certified diabetes educator at Boston's Joslin Clinic. However, because people with diabetes need to factor in the effect of each meal on their blood sugar levels, she recommends that you consult an RD before starting any diet. Your RD can help you adapt a diet to your specific needs and culinary skills, and can guide you in making the changes needed to take weight off. In fact, working with an RD can actually make your diet *more* effective: One study found that people with diabetes who met with a dietitian even occasionally over the course of a year lost more weight, needed fewer diabetes medications, and had a better quality of life than those who did not (*Diabetes Care*, July 2004).

Of course, losing pounds *sensibly* is the key to achieving and maintaining a healthy weight. As your RD will tell you, you shouldn't try to drop a lot of weight quickly through fad diets or supplements, since you're likely to gain back any weight you lose and then some. And it's still not clear how low-carb, high-protein diets influence diabetes (see box on page 41). Instead, set realistic goals: Remember, losing just 10 to 15 pounds can help significantly lower your blood sugar. Here are some key things to keep in mind when attempting to slim down.

DR. WEIL SAYS: "You're more likely to succeed at managing your weight if you do it *for yourself*, to feel healthier and not to meet others' expectations. Success is also more likely if you concentrate on gradually adopting healthier habits and maintaining them for the long term. Congratulate yourself for each walk you take, each fruit or vegetable you eat, or each time you manage your 'emotional' hunger in ways other than food."

Your meds may cause weight gain. Extra weight can increase insulin resistance, worsening diabetes. But, unfortunately, some diabetes treatments aimed at lowering blood sugar can also make you gain weight. For example, insulin, as well as oral diabetes drugs like sulfonylureas and thiazolidine-diones, can cause you to put on extra pounds. Some people may try to lower their doses of these medications to stave off weight gain, but that's a dangerous move that can lead to high blood sugar and increase your risk of dia-

Jury Still Out on Low-Carb Diets

Since carbohydrates can raise blood sugar, a low-carb diet might be even better for people with diabetes, right? Not necessarily, says Jo-Anne Rizzotto. Low-carb, high-protein diets (such as the Atkins diet) restrict the amount of rice, pasta, certain fruits and vegetables, and other carbs that you can eat, while encouraging you to fill your plate with more meat, poultry, and other high-protein foods, which they claim will kick-start your metabolism. More specifically, these diets are based on the idea that eating fewer carbs decreases circulating levels of the hormone insulin and triggers a state called ketosis, in which your body burns fat, rather than carbs, as fuel.

Like most diets, Atkins and similar plans *can* lead to weight loss, at least in the short term, because people are eating fewer calories. And some studies have found that such diets can increase insulin sensitivity, improve cholesterol levels, and lower A1C levels in people with diabetes, presumably by limiting carbs. But Rizzotto worries that low-carb diets may provide too much protein for some people with diabetes: There have been no long-term studies looking at the effects of excessive protein intake, which can be a concern for people with diabetes-related kidney problems. Plus, these diets may not provide enough vitamins, minerals, fiber, and other protective compounds that are important parts of a healthy diet, especially for people with diabetes. If you want to try a low-carb diet, Rizzotto recommends checking with your doctor or RD first, who can review the plan and make any adjustments for your particular needs.

betes-related complications. Instead, talk with your doctor, who may be able to switch your medication or add another oral diabetes drug like metformin (which can cause weight loss in some people) to neutralize this side effect.

A healthy diet helps. Foods like whole grains, beans, and fruits and vegetables tend to be filling and low in calories. They're also excellent sources of fiber and complex carbohydrates, which can help stabilize your blood sugar. Avoid refined carbohydrates (foods made with sugar and flour), which can spike blood sugar and are now believed to be major dietary contributors to obesity. And drink lots of water: It has no calories, is filling, and is more healthful than diet soda or alcoholic beverages, which can be loaded with calories. (See Chapter Three for more on healthy eating and diabetes.)

DR. WEIL SAYS: "If you want to try a low-carb diet, I would avoid the Atkins diet and look at more sensible eating plans like The Zone and South Beach diets."

Calories count. For a week or two, estimate your average daily caloric intake by consulting food labels or calorie-counter books. This will give you a clearer picture of how much you're eating and can help you learn how much your body really needs to be healthy and satisfied. When trying to lose weight, women should go no lower than 1,200 calories a day, men no lower than 1,500 calories, to ensure adequate nutrition. Your RD may give you more specific goals geared to your individual situation.

A food diary can be useful. Writing down what you eat can make you more mindful of your eating habits and keep you honest. For a few weeks or more, try recording every food and beverage you consume, the portion size, and when you consumed it. Many people also find that keeping track of their physical activity helps them keep moving and stay motivated. You might try combining this information with your daily log of blood sugar readings to get an idea of how certain foods and activities affect them.

Portions are important. Reading labels can help, but at first you may want to measure foods and even weigh them until you become a better judge of portion size. See box on page 38 for more.

Mindfulness matters. If you're not paying attention to what you're putting in your mouth, it's easy to overeat. Don't watch TV or read the newspaper while you eat. Chew your food thoroughly, and practice putting your fork or spoon down between bites. Eating mindfully can help you enjoy your food more and feel satisfied sooner.

Emotional eating can contribute calories. The stress of living with diabetes may make you reach for food when you're feeling down rather than eating because you feel hungry. Instead, do the Relaxing Breath exercise (see page 46) or try progressive muscle relaxation (page 45). By the time you finish, your craving may well have passed.

Exercise makes a difference. Burning calories through physical activity is an essential part of any successful weight-loss (and weight-maintenance) program, and can also help lower your blood sugar. For more on exercise, see Chapter Four.

CHAPTER SIX

Stress Less

By now, you probably know enough about diabetes to understand how certain foods, regular activity, and the amount you weigh affect your blood sugar. But did you know that the stress you feel can cause blood sugar levels to rise? Just as a stressful situation—be it the unwanted stress of financial difficulties or the fear of public speaking—can spike your blood pressure, it can also raise blood *sugar*. That might sound odd, but the connection isn't as strange as you might think.

In fact, the link makes perfect sense, says Richard Surwit, PhD, co-director of the Behavioral Endocrinology Clinic at Duke University Medical Center in Durham, North Carolina. Dr. Surwit, who has studied the effect of stress on diabetes for decades, points out that some of the same hormones are responsible for influencing both stress levels and blood sugar levels. In other words, the hormones your body releases when it's faced with a stressful situation can also have an affect on your blood sugar. Fortunately, by managing the stress in your life you can help bring down your blood sugar, as you'll learn in this chapter.

The Science of Stress

Have you ever found yourself cornered by a hungry tiger? Probably not, unless you're a zookeeper. The truth is, your body can't tell the difference between the threat of being eaten alive by a scary beast and stress that's more along the lines of a looming deadline at work. As far as your nervous system is concerned, the source of stress doesn't really make much difference. That's because your body reacts to work worries, traffic jams, com-

"There cannot be a stressful crisis next week. My schedule is already full."

HENRY KISSINGER

puter snafus, and other modern stresses in much the same way it did when your prehistoric ancestors were being chased by predators.

When you're feeling stressed, your body pumps out hormones such as adrenaline and cortisol, which increase your heart rate, blood pressure, and muscle tension, a reaction that's meant to help you either run away from danger or stay and battle it. This is called the fight-or-flight response, and you'll experience it whether you're contending with a tiger or your boss.

> **DR. WEIL SAYS:** "It's easy to think that external 'stressors'—a demanding boss, an unhappy spouse, mounting bills—are the cause of your tensions, but, in fact, you have a choice as to how they affect you, and you can learn to change your reactions to them."

You may feel and possibly recognize the effects of stress hormones like cortisol and adrenaline on your body. Your heart pounds, your breathing gets faster and shallower, and your muscles might feel tense. But cortisol and adrenaline can also affect your body in ways that are less obvious. They trigger your liver to convert energy reserves (carbohydrates and protein that are stored by your body) into glucose and release it into the blood. If that tiger really trapped you, this energy would give you the boost needed to head for the hills or stay behind and fight.

In most people, the pancreas moves that glucose into cells by releasing insulin. But when you have diabetes, the cells are either resistant to insulin or the pancreas can't release enough of it. This means that the glucose stays in your blood, resulting in high blood sugar levels. So, you can see how

Try This: Stress and Blood Sugar

Does stress influence *your* blood sugar? Here's an easy way to find out: Next time you check your blood glucose, take a minute to assess your stress before you test. Rate your emotional stress on a scale of 1 to 10, with 1 representing none and 10 being extreme. Then test your blood sugar and write down both numbers in your logbook. After a few weeks, you'll probably start to notice a pattern, with high stress levels corresponding to high blood sugar readings and vice versa.

Try This: Progressive Muscle Relaxation

This simple mind-body technique, known as progressive muscle relaxation (PMR), has been shown in studies by Drs. Surwit and Feinglos to help lower stress—and blood sugar—when practiced regularly by people with diabetes. Try this exercise sitting comfortably.

- Close your eyes and concentrate on your breathing for a few seconds. Now focus on a single body part or muscle group, say, your right foot.

- While taking a deep inhaling breath, tense the muscles in your right foot— not to the point of pain—and hold for 3 to 5 seconds. Then slowly relax the foot as you exhale and let stress flow from your body.

- Continue this tense and release sequence as you move up the right leg to the calves and thighs, then to the left foot, and gradually to the buttocks, abdomen, each arm, shoulders, and face.

- Finally, scan the body for any unresolved tension. Practice PMR for 10 to 15 minutes each day, or when time is limited, try a shortened version by doing the lower body, upper body, and face.

stress, whether it's the acute anxiety of a fender-bender or the longer-lasting stress of marital troubles, can and does affect diabetes. In fact, even so-called good stress—like cheering on your favorite baseball team or riding a roller coaster—can boost blood sugar, although these short bursts of excitement are believed to be less harmful than the chronic stresses described earlier. Fortunately, relaxation techniques such as those discussed below can help ease chronic stress and even lower your blood sugar in the process.

Relaxation to the Rescue

Since stress can have negative effects on blood sugar, it stands to reason that the reverse would also be true. Indeed, regularly practicing stress reduction measures will help lower blood sugar and improve your control over diabetes. That's the finding of several studies by Drs. Surwit and Feinglos, both of Duke University Medical Center. They've discovered that when people with diabetes learn and regularly practice relaxation techniques like deep breathing, mental imagery, and progressive muscle relaxation (alternately tensing and relaxing the body's muscle groups), their blood sugar levels significantly improve. In one study of 108 people with diabetes, for example, they found that after one year nearly a third of those who regularly practiced such stress reduction techniques lowered their A1C readings by at least one percentage point (*Diabetes Care*, January 2002). At first, that doesn't sound like much. But it's an even bigger change than you might expect to get from taking some oral diabetes drugs.

Stress reduction techniques work by helping to lower levels of stress hormones like cortisol, which in turn decreases blood sugar. Although most forms of stress reduction appear to be effective, Dr. Surwit says he's seen the best results with progressive muscle relaxation (PMR). This simple approach is easy to learn, requires no special equipment, and costs nothing. Breath work, such as Dr. Weil's Relaxing Breath, may also make a difference. If you find yourself easily stressed, consider practicing one of these techniques on a regular basis. (For instructions, see page 45 and 46.)

The Diabetes and Depression Link

It's not unusual to find that having diabetes might make you feel down from time to time. Living with a chronic disease can make anyone feel blue

Try This: The Relaxing Breath

Dr. Weil's yoga-derived Relaxing Breath is an effective and time-efficient relaxation method that you can use instead of or in addition to progressive muscle relaxation. Try it for yourself and see if this breathing exercise produces a pleasant altered state and helps relieve stress.

1. Sit or lie comfortably with your back straight, and place your tongue in what's called the yogic position: Touch the tip of your tongue to the back of your upper front teeth and slide it up until it rests on the bony ridge of tissue between your teeth and palate. Keep your tongue there for the duration of the exercise.

2. Exhale completely and loudly through your mouth.

3. Close your mouth lightly. Inhale through your nose quietly to the count of 4.

4. Hold your breath for a count of 7.

5. Exhale audibly through your mouth to the count of 8. If you have difficulty exhaling with your tongue in place, try pursing your lips.

6. Repeat steps 3 through 5 three more times, for a total of four cycles. Breathe normally and notice how your body feels.

The key to doing this exercise is maintaining the 4-7-8 ratio, ensuring that your exhalation is twice as long as your inhalation. It doesn't matter how fast or slow you count; your pace will be determined by how long you can comfortably hold your breath.

Practice this exercise at least twice a day, preferably when you first wake up and before you go to sleep, or just before meditating. After a month of practice, you can increase the number of breath cycles to eight. This exercise is safe for everyone, although people with chronic obstructive pulmonary disease (COPD) or other respiratory problems may not wish to hold their breath for too long while doing the Relaxing Breath; just count at a pace that feels comfortable to you while still maintaining the 4-7-8 ratio.

sometimes. But clinical depression—feeling persistently sad or disinterested in everyday activities for more than two weeks—is also common in people with diabetes. Scientists aren't sure why, but research shows that people with diabetes have higher rates of depression than those without the disease. It's not entirely clear whether having diabetes makes people more depressed or if depression itself raises the risk, but evidence suggests that both may be the case. For instance, some studies have found that people who are depressed or have a history of depression have twice the risk of developing type 2 diabetes. More research is needed, but it may be that stress hormones like adrenaline and cortisol—which appear to be higher in chronically depressed people—raise glucose levels. If these levels stay elevated, diabetes can often result. Plus, people who are depressed may not eat well or exercise, which could also raise their risk of diabetes.

On the other hand, simply having diabetes can make you feel depressed. In fact, studies indicate that people with diabetes—especially those who also have complications of the disease—may be up to four times as likely to be depressed as people without the disease. That may be because coping with the frustration and unpredictability of diabetes can make you feel helpless, a common trigger of depression.

Whatever the connection between diabetes and depression, the point is that treatment can make a difference in both instances. Research has found that both cognitive-behavioral therapy (CBT) and antidepressant medications can help ease depression and get diabetes under control. In CBT, a therapist will teach you how to recognize self-defeating thoughts ("I'll never be able to control my diabetes") and replace them with positive statements that encourage you to take better care of yourself ("I want to stay healthy and active"). By reframing your negative thought patterns and helping you see them in a different light, CBT can yield real results. For example, one study of 51 people with both type 2 diabetes and major depression showed that 85 percent of those who received 10 weeks of individual CBT achieved remission from depression, compared with just 27 percent of control subjects. An added bonus: People who received CBT also had lower A1C scores six months after treatment (*Annals of Internal Medicine*, October 15, 1998). Other studies have found that treating depression with antidepressant drugs can relieve this mood disorder, which can also improve blood sugar levels in people with diabetes. If you think you may be depressed, ask your doctor for a referral to a therapist or contact the National Association of Cognitive-Behavioral Therapists at *www.nacbt.org* or *(800) 853-1135*.

Anger Management

Having diabetes may make you angry—at yourself, at your loved ones, at doctors, or even at the disease itself. Anger can be healthy, if you can channel that energy into taking care of yourself properly. But when getting hot under the collar keeps you from following your treatment plan or starts to affect your relationships with others, it's worth seeking professional help. Diabetes may also affect your emotions in another way: Losing your temper for no real reason can be a symptom of blood sugar that's too low (hypoglycemia). If you think this may be true for you, try to use a burst of anger as a signal to check your blood sugar and treat it if it's too low.

"Diabetes Burnout"

There's a certain kind of stress that comes from the daily grind of living with a chronic disease like diabetes and needing to be conscious of your health habits on a regular basis. That type of stress is hard to avoid and control, and you may start to feel burnt out and overwhelmed, like you just don't have the time or energy to take good care of yourself. It's easy to see why this happens. Whether you've just been diagnosed with diabetes or have been coping with the disease for years, you may eventually come to a point when you no longer feel motivated to deal with the constant demands of good self-care. You feel burnt out and burdened by the responsibilities that come from having diabetes. That's understandable. But ignoring the problem will only make it worse in the long run: Neglecting to take good care of yourself can cause blood sugar to get too high and can increase your risk of diabetes-related complications.

Stress reduction techniques can help. Better still, you may want to visit your certified diabetes educator (CDE) or physician, who can help you brainstorm ways to renew your energies, re-evaluate your priorities, and make your treatment plan easier to follow. You might also consider joining a support group, where you'll meet other people who have diabetes and learn how they manage the condition. (You can find live support groups at hospitals and community centers or online through the Internet; see the Resource Guide on page 74 for more.) Seeing a therapist or a special counselor called a health psychologist who is trained to help you deal with the emotional aspects of living with diabetes may also be useful in coping with burnout.

DR. WEIL SAYS: "The word *stress* comes from the same Latin word that gives us *strict*, which originally meant 'narrow' or 'tight.' Stress is the discomfort or distress caused by forces that limit our freedom and movement."

CHAPTER SEVEN

Selecting Supplements

hether you use insulin, take other medications, or manage your diabetes with lifestyle measures alone, you may wonder whether dietary supplements can also keep your blood sugar under control. Truth is, certain supplements can help. In fact, they're being recommended as adjunctive treatments for diabetes by integrative physicians as well as some conventional endocrinologists, says Randy Horwitz, MD, medical director of the University of Arizona's Program in Integrative Medicine.

It makes sense that some supplements appear to benefit people with diabetes: Your body depends on a range of vitamins, minerals, and other nutrients to regulate blood sugar. When levels of one of these nutrients, such as chromium, fall too low, your blood sugar can rise. On the other hand, research shows that supplementing with chromium can help lower blood sugar. Other supplements, like the herbs ginseng and fenugreek, have also been shown to improve blood sugar and insulin sensitivity, although the reasons why still aren't clear.

In this chapter, you'll read about these and other popular supplements typically suggested for people with diabetes. The supplements backed by the best research and most recommended by Dr. Weil and our other experts are marked with a star (★). Others may also be helpful but appear to work similarly to each other. If you'd like to try supplements, start with one or more of the items that are starred and see how blood sugar improves; if it's still high, consider adding one of the other supplements mentioned here. Remember, though, that supplements shouldn't replace diet, exercise, stress reduction, and other lifestyle approaches for diabetes. And if you are

> ## "In all things of nature there is something of the marvelous."
>
> ARISTOTLE

on medications, be sure to tell your doctor what supplements you take, since he or she may need to adjust your doses. (Also, kids, as well as women who are pregnant or breastfeeding, shouldn't take these supplements because it isn't clear how they affect developing fetuses and small children.)

★ **Alpha-lipoic acid (ALA).** Although this compound is made in the body in trace amounts and used in the conversion of food to energy, additional ALA supplements may help quench free radicals and reduce oxidative stress. This tiny molecule recycles antioxidants such as vitamins C and E, prolonging their effectiveness, and appears to enhance the uptake of glucose into cells, making them more responsive to insulin. It's also been shown to improve symptoms of diabetic neuropathy (see page 59), possibly by promoting blood flow to the nerves.

HOW TO TAKE ► Take up to 400 mg of ALA a day for diabetes; you can take up to 800 mg daily if you already have neuropathy.

POSSIBLE CONCERNS ► ALA appears to be free of side effects, but tell your doctor that you're taking it, so your glucose levels can be monitored more closely and your diabetes or neuropathy medications adjusted, if necessary.

MAY BE BEST FOR ► Anyone with diabetes, but especially those who have peripheral neuropathy.

★ **Chromium.** This mineral may make it easier for insulin to bind to cells by increasing the number of insulin receptors on them. As a result, cells become more sensitive to insulin and more glucose moves out of the bloodstream and into the cells. Studies show that animals fed a chromium-deficient diet have high blood sugar. Likewise, human research suggests that people with a milder form of chromium deficiency can develop impaired glucose tolerance, also known as prediabetes. While studies of chromium supplementation are mixed, most research has found that people with diabetes or prediabetes who take this mineral, in doses ranging from 150 to 1,000 mcg daily, have improved glucose tolerance and lower blood sugar levels than those not taking it.

HOW TO TAKE ► Brewer's yeast, wheat germ, and chicken are foods that are rich in chromium, but if you have diabetes or prediabetes, your best bet is to supplement with up to 1,000 mcg daily of this mineral. Choose capsules or tablets of GTF (glucose tolerance factor) chromium, the form that's best used by the body.

POSSIBLE CONCERNS ► Lab and animal studies suggest that very high doses of chromium picolinate, another form of this mineral, may cause DNA damage that could increase the risk of cancer. It's still unclear whether these same mutations would occur in humans taking typical doses of the supplement. GTF chromium hasn't been linked to the same risks. (By the way, despite manufacturers' claims, there's not much good scientific evidence to support the use of chromium as a weight loss aid or to improve athletic performance.)

MAY BE BEST FOR▶ Anyone with diabetes or prediabetes, when taken at recommended doses.

★ **Ginseng.** Although there are several different varieties of this herb, American ginseng (*Panax quinquefolius*) appears to be the most helpful form for people with diabetes. Researchers aren't yet sure how ginseng lowers blood sugar but suspect that it may slow the breakdown of carbohydrates into glucose, control the secretion of insulin from the pancreas, and help move glucose into cells. More research is needed, but early studies have found that people with diabetes who take ginseng have lower blood sugar levels than those who do not.

HOW TO TAKE▶ Look for American ginseng products standardized for ginsenosides, believed to be the active ingredients, and take 200 to 600 mg a day. It may be best to take this herb in divided doses, prior to or with meals: In one small, short-term study, researchers found that people taking American ginseng about 40 minutes before eating reduced the rise in blood sugar that typically occurs after meals (*Archives of Internal Medicine*, April 10, 2000).

POSSIBLE CONCERNS▶ Side effects and adverse reactions don't generally occur with American ginseng, although it may cause nervousness in some people and may intensify the blood-thinning effects of the drug Coumadin.

MAY BE BEST FOR▶ People with diabetes who notice that their blood sugar levels typically spike after a meal.

★ **Magnesium.** Like chromium, this mineral helps move glucose into cells, possibly by increasing the body's ability to produce more insulin. Research has found that diets low in magnesium increase the odds of insulin resistance and that people who have low blood levels of magnesium are at higher risk for diabetes. Some experts theorize that the link between a diet that's rich in whole grains, nuts, and green leafy vegetables and a reduced risk of diabetes is because these foods are good sources of magne-

Q&A

Can taking glucosamine supplements for arthritis raise my blood sugar?

Probably not. There's been a theoretical concern, based on some small studies in animals, that glucosamine (an amino sugar) may possibly affect insulin resistance, but a more recent study in humans found no such effect (*Archives of Internal Medicine*, July 13, 2003). Still, it's a good idea to monitor your blood glucose levels more carefully when taking this supplement for osteoarthritis.

sium. Still, evidence about the effect of magnesium *supplements* on diabetes control is mixed, although some studies show a decrease in blood sugar in people taking them.

HOW TO TAKE ▸ Eat plenty of whole grains, as well as nuts and bananas, which are also good sources of magnesium. It's also reasonable for most people with diabetes to supplement with 400 mg daily of magnesium glycinate, a form that's better absorbed by the body.

POSSIBLE CONCERNS ▸ Magnesium may cause diarrhea, so you may want to take it with twice as much calcium (which can be constipating) to counteract this effect. Also, people with kidney failure shouldn't take magnesium supplements without a doctor's approval, since they're at risk for accumulating high blood levels of this mineral, a potentially fatal problem that can also cause heart arrhythmias and low blood pressure.

MAY BE BEST FOR ▸ People with diabetes or prediabetes but without kidney problems who consume few magnesium-rich foods.

★ **Vitamin E.** Blood sugar levels that are consistently high can trigger increased activity of free radicals, dangerous compounds that cause oxidative stress, which may damage DNA and weaken immunity. Antioxidants like vitamin E neutralize free radicals, possibly helping to prevent long-term diabetes complications like heart disease, which is also linked to oxidative stress. Plus, some research has found that vitamin E may have a direct effect on diabetes control, since some people who supplement with it tend to have lower blood sugar levels.

HOW TO TAKE ▸ Aim for 400 to 800 IU of natural vitamin E (or 80 mg of mixed tocopherols and tocotrienols) daily. Vitamin E may work best when taken as part of a daily antioxidant regimen that also includes 200 mg of vitamin C, 15,000 IU of mixed carotenoids, and 200 mcg of selenium.

POSSIBLE CONCERNS ▸ This supplement may increase the blood-thinning effects of the drug Coumadin.

MAY BE BEST FOR ▸ Anyone with diabetes or prediabetes, especially those already taking a daily antioxidant formula.

In addition to the supplements above, you may want to consider experimenting with the following four herbs. Choose one and give it a good two-month trial to see how it works for you.

Bitter melon. Long used by herbalists as a treatment for diabetes, this fruit (*Momordica charantia*) contains compounds that are believed to have properties that help fight the disease. Bitter melon lowers blood sugar and A1C levels in people with diabetes. Although it's unclear how bitter melon actually does this, researchers suspect that it may increase the secretion of insulin.

HOW TO TAKE ▶ You can drink bitter melon juice to treat diabetes, but it lives up to its bitter name. Instead, look for standardized extracts in capsule form and take 100 to 200 mg three times a day.

POSSIBLE CONCERNS ▶ Bitter melon may compound the effects of diabetes drugs, causing blood sugar to drop too low (hypoglycemia), so be sure to tell your doctor before taking this herb.

Gurmar. The Hindi name for this herb (*Gymnema sylvestre*) means "destroyer of sugar" because it blocks sweet tastes when placed on the tongue. Practitioners of ayurvedic (Indian) medicine traditionally use gurmar to treat diabetes, and it's thought that the herb helps enhance the pancreas's production of insulin. There haven't been many studies on gurmar, but those done suggest that people with diabetes who take it as a supplement in addition to conventional treatment have better blood sugar control than those who do not.

HOW TO TAKE ▶ Take 200 mg twice a day of a standardized gurmar extract.

POSSIBLE CONCERNS ▶ People who are allergic to milkweed and other related plants may also react to gurmar.

Fenugreek. The seeds of this legume (*Trigonella foenum*) related to the chickpea are valued in ayurvedic medicine for their blood-sugar-lowering effects. Some studies have found that people taking fenugreek have better blood sugar control than those who don't take this supplement. It's not clear how fenugreek helps lower blood sugar, although it may increase the number of insulin receptors on cells.

HOW TO TAKE ▶ Look for fenugreek seed powder in capsule form and take 2.5 grams twice a day.

POSSIBLE CONCERNS ▶ High doses may cause diarrhea and gas, and your urine may develop a maple-syrup smell after you take fenugreek; this is a harmless change.

DR. WEIL SAYS: "A surprising number of plants used in traditional medicine throughout the world show hypoglycemic activity—that is, they help lower elevated blood sugar. Let your physician know if you're experimenting with these herbal remedies, in case your prescribed diabetes medications need adjustment."

Prickly pear. Found in desert locales from the southwestern United States to Australia, extracts of this cactus (*Opuntia streptacantha*) have long been used in Latin American countries as a treatment for diabetes. More research is needed, but human studies suggest that prickly pear cactus, also known as nopal, may lower blood sugar and enhance insulin sensitivity, perhaps because of its high soluble fiber content.

HOW TO TAKE ▶ Look for standardized extracts and follow package directions.

POSSIBLE CONCERNS ▶ Prickly pear may compound the effects of diabetes drugs, causing blood sugar to drop too low (hypoglycemia), so be sure to tell your doctor before taking this herb.

What about . . .

Caiapo. This extract from the skin of a white sweet potato native to Brazil has been shown in preliminary studies to lower blood sugar and A1C levels, possibly by improving insulin sensitivity. Caiapo is sold as a dietary supplement for diabetes in Japan, but isn't currently available in the United States.

Vanadium. This nutrient was used to help control diabetes before insulin was discovered in the early 1920s, and some small studies have shown it to lower blood sugar in people with diabetes. However, because of its numerous side effects—including diarrhea, cramping, nausea, vomiting, and gas—and its possible link to liver and kidney disease, vanadium is no longer recommended by most experts.

CHAPTER EIGHT

Coping with Complications

Having high blood sugar doesn't mean that the effects of diabetes are limited to your blood; such complications can be more far-reaching and widespread. When blood sugar is consistently elevated, it can damage blood vessels and nerves, causing or contributing to problems ranging from memory loss and heart disease to blindness and loss of a limb. Diabetes can affect your entire body, from your head straight down to your toes.

That may sound scary. In fact, both Program in Integrative Medicine medical director Randy Horwitz, MD, and Duke University Medical Center endocrinologist Mark Feinglos, MD, say that the top concern of their patients with diabetes is the threat of such complications. But the good news is that you can greatly reduce your risk of developing these and other problems by keeping your blood sugar levels as close to normal as possible. Good diabetes control can also help to slow complications that may have already begun. And there's good evidence that even small changes can make a big difference: The large United Kingdom Prospective Diabetes Study has found that people with diabetes who keep their A1C levels to 7 percent or below suffer much less damage to their bodies than those whose A1C stays closer to 8 percent.

> "The biggest problem in the world could have been solved when it was small."
>
> LAO TZU

How Damage Happens

High blood sugar levels are directly responsible for diabetes-related complications: They can cause your blood vessels to become narrower, less flexible, or clogged, making it harder for blood to get to vital organs like the heart, brain, eyes, and kidneys. High blood sugar can damage your nerves, too, although it's still not clear how this damage occurs.

Over time, such damage can create health problems for people with diabetes, putting them at much higher risk for conditions like heart disease, stroke, vision loss, kidney problems, and Alzheimer's disease. Diabetes also increases the odds of neuropathy, nerve damage that can make it difficult to feel certain parts of your body, typically the hands and feet. When you lack sensation in your feet, you're more likely to injure them and develop infections. Because people with diabetes heal more slowly, this can increase the chances of infections so severe they necessitate surgery or even amputation.

It can take many years for complications to develop, so if you're newly diagnosed with diabetes and feeling fine, you should take advantage of this time to prevent them. This is even more important for children and young adults, who are more likely to develop such complications at much earlier ages. Even if you have them when you're first diagnosed, keeping your blood sugar levels low and following the tips here can help you treat symptoms early on and prevent them from worsening.

Cardiovascular Disease

Having diabetes can harm your heart in several ways. First, high levels of glucose in the blood can cause blood vessels to stiffen and clog over time, a condition known as atherosclerosis. In addition, diabetes can make you more prone to high cholesterol and high blood pressure, which can also damage blood vessels. And having diabetes causes your platelets to produce more of a substance that increases blood clotting. These problems can up your chances of having angina (chest pain), intermittent claudication (decreased circulation and pain in the legs), a heart attack, or stroke. In fact, simply having diabetes makes you up to four times more likely to have a heart attack and five times more likely to have a stroke than people without it.

Your doctor should regularly screen you for cardiovascular disease by checking what are often referred to as your ABCs. "A" is for A1C, which, as you learned in Chapter Two, should be below 7 percent. "B" stands for blood pressure; yours should be below 120/80 mmHg. And "C" refers to cholesterol, which should be less than 80 mg/dl for LDL ("bad") and more than 45 mg/dl for HDL ("good") cholesterol. Your doctor will determine how often to check your ABCs. If your numbers are too high, you may be

A Guide to Diabetes Complications from Head to Toe

Diabetes is a disease that can have whole-body effects. Keep in mind, though, that not everyone with diabetes will develop all (or any) of these complications, especially if you keep blood sugar at healthy levels.

Mouth ▸ Poorly controlled diabetes can cause severe gum disease, which in turn can contribute to cardiovascular problems.

Lungs ▸ People with poorly controlled diabetes may have increased breathing problems: The higher their sugar levels, the worse their lungs appear to function, according to one study.

Gastrointestinal tract ▸ Diabetes-related neuropathy can affect the gastro-intestinal tract, resulting in symptoms like bloating, diarrhea, or constipation. Plus, people with diabetes have about three times the normal risk of developing colorectal cancer, possibly because these diseases share similar lifestyle factors.

Skin ▸ Diabetes can make your skin dry and itchy and raises the risk of fungal and other infections.

Genitals ▸ Men with diabetes are more likely to suffer erectile dysfunction (impotence), while women may have trouble with vaginal dryness and achieving orgasm, due to decreased blood flow to the genitals. High blood sugar also raises the odds of yeast infections.

Feet ▸ Nerve damage to the feet from high blood sugar can dull sensation there, putting you at risk for injuries and infections. More than 60 percent of nontraumatic lower limb amputations in the United States occur among people with diabetes.

Brain ▸ Diabetes raises the risk of Alzheimer's disease and other forms of dementia by up to 65 percent in older people.

Eyes ▸ Complications like diabetic retinopathy and glaucoma make diabetes the leading cause of blindness in adults under age 75.

Heart ▸ People with diabetes are up to four times more likely to develop heart disease and five times more likely to suffer a stroke than those without this condition. Heart disease is the leading cause of death in people with diabetes.

Liver ▸ Diabetes can trigger nonalcoholic steatohepatitis (NASH), a fatty infiltration and inflammation of the liver that can damage this organ, especially in overweight people. An increased risk of liver cancer has also been linked to diabetes.

Kidneys ▸ High blood sugar can damage the kidneys, leading to impaired function (nephropathy) and, over time, kidney failure.

Bladder ▸ Neuropathy can also affect the bladder, leading to incontinence and increased urinary tract infections.

Immunity ▸ High blood sugar makes white blood cells work more slowly, increasing the risk of infections of the mouth, skin, bladder, genitals, ears, lungs, and feet. Diabetes also ups the risk and severity of flu and pneumonia.

placed on a cholesterol-lowering statin drug, low-dose aspirin therapy, or other medications to help get them under control. But whether or not you already have heart disease, the following steps can help prevent it and keep it from worsening.

Don't smoke. The nicotine in cigarettes constricts your blood vessels in the same way that diabetes does, increasing risk for a heart attack. Quitting smoking is the single most important thing you can do to lessen this risk.

Eat well. The diet you follow for diabetes (see Chapter Three) can serve double duty by helping to control blood sugar levels *and* protecting against heart disease. To promote heart health, make sure it's low in saturated and trans fats, processed foods, and animal products. And you'll want it to include foods high in monounsaturated fats and omega-3 fatty acids, as well as whole grains and fresh fruits and vegetables.

Exercise regularly. A sedentary lifestyle is one of the most common risk factors for heart disease. Being physically active not only helps lower your blood sugar, but also helps decrease LDL and raise HDL cholesterol. It has other heart benefits too, such as lowering blood pressure and keeping blood vessels flexible. And it also protects your cardiovascular system by making it easier to cope with stress and shed pounds.

Try This: Taking Care of Your Feet

If diabetes has caused nerve damage or poor circulation in your feet, you may lose sensation in them. That means it can be difficult to tell if your shoes don't fit properly or if you've got a pebble in your sock, for example. Since you can't feel these sources of discomfort, you can easily develop blisters, abrasions, or other foot injuries without knowing it. Left unchecked, such problems can turn into foot ulcers that become infected, sometimes requiring surgery. The best way to avoid such concerns is to keep blood sugar levels healthy, take good care of your feet, and check them every day for blisters, cuts, and other problems. (Your doctor should also examine your feet at each visit.) Good foot care can reduce your risk of leg or foot amputation by up to 85 percent.

- Wash your feet every day with mild soap and warm water (test it with your hand or an elbow first to make sure it's not too hot). Dry them carefully and apply lotion everywhere but between your toes.

- Examine your feet daily. Look for red or swollen areas, for blisters, and for cuts. Use a hand mirror to see the bottoms of your feet or ask a loved one for help if you need it.

- Cut toenails straight across and gently file the edges.

- Wear comfortable shoes that fit (see page 30 for shopping tips) and always wear socks. Never walk barefoot, especially outdoors.

- Leave serious foot care to the professionals: Don't treat or remove calluses, corns, warts, or other problems at home. Let a podiatrist or your doctor handle them.

Maintain a healthy weight. You know that extra pounds, especially around your midsection, contribute to diabetes, and they can also strain your heart and increase the chances of developing high blood pressure and high cholesterol. Modest weight loss—losing just 5 to 10 percent of your current weight by following the advice in Chapter Five—can help lower your risk of heart disease.

> **DR. WEIL SAYS:** "Diabetes affects every organ in the body, causing symptoms ranging from blindness to impotence. This is definitely a disease you want to control to avoid complications."

Neuropathy

Although it's not clear exactly how, chronically high blood sugar can damage your nerves—a condition known as diabetic neuropathy, which occurs in up to 70 percent of people with the disease. Neuropathy can sometimes affect internal organs like the intestine, bladder, and heart, leading to gastrointestinal woes, incontinence, and irregular heartbeat. But the most common type of neuropathy is peripheral neuropathy (PN), which causes pain and numbness in the extremities, typically the hands and feet. In areas that are affected, you may feel pins-and-needles sensations, alternating with bouts of burning pain. This can make it difficult to walk, sleep, or hold things.

The best way to prevent PN and keep it from worsening is to stabilize your blood sugar and, therefore, control diabetes. There's no cure for PN, although over-the-counter pain relievers like acetaminophen, aspirin, and ibuprofen can ease discomfort somewhat. Your doctor may also prescribe an antidepressant or antiseizure drug, since these medications appear to block PN-related pain. The natural measures here may also help.

Use capsaicin. This hot pepper extract seems to ease symptoms of PN by depleting a substance that transmits pain signals. Apply a 0.025 percent over-the-counter cream (such as Zostrix) to painful areas up to three times a day. Don't apply it to broken skin, and wash your hands after use.

Try supplements. Program in Integrative Medicine graduate Associate Fellow Victoria Rommel, MD, says her patients with diabetes have found alpha-lipoic acid (ALA) particularly helpful for treating neuropathy (see

Chapter Seven for more). Work your way up to taking no more than 400 mg of ALA twice a day, since higher doses may cause stomach upset.

Vitamins B-1, B-6, and B-12 are also important to proper nerve function. Take a B-50 B-complex supplement daily. (Make sure your B-complex supplement or multivitamin does not contain more than 100 mg of vitamin B-6, as higher doses can actually cause symptoms of neuropathy.)

Experiment. Some people have had luck using magnetic foot insoles for PN, while others prefer acupuncture or reflexology (which involves hands-on pressure to points on the foot or hand). You can experiment with these measures to see if they work for you.

Vision Problems

Diabetes is the leading cause of new cases of blindness among adults aged 20 to 74. The following conditions are two of the main reasons for this.

Diabetic retinopathy. About one-third of people with diabetes have diabetic retinopathy, a vision problem that occurs when high blood sugar levels damage vessels in the eye, causing them to leak blood and fat. People with diabetic retinopathy can have blurry vision and blind spots, and 5 to

Help for HHS

Whether you manage your diabetes with oral medications, insulin, or lifestyle measures alone, you should know about an acute complication called hyperosmolar hyperglycemic state (HHS). This potentially fatal problem occurs mainly in people with type 2 diabetes, typically those over age 65. HHS is a gradual process in which blood sugar levels can eventually soar as high as 1,000 mg/dl (126 mg/dl is considered normal for people with diabetes). It has a variety of causes, including stress, untreated infection, certain medications, and even not drinking enough water, a common problem in older people. If you develop HHS, your blood sugar will rise higher and higher over a period of days or weeks and you'll find yourself feeling thirsty all the time and urinating more. Untreated, HHS can lead to seizures, coma, and death, but you can prevent this serious complication with the following steps.

Check blood sugar often. HHS often happens in people who aren't well aware of their blood sugar levels. Even checking once a day (more often if you're sick) can clue you in to the risk of HHS before it occurs.

Drink plenty of fluids. Caffeine- and alcohol-free beverages like water will keep you hydrated, lowering your chances of HHS.

Check your meds. Steroids, diuretics, antiseizure drugs, beta blockers, and Tagamet (for heartburn) can all raise blood sugar. Ask your doctor about possible substitutions.

Watch for symptoms. Call your doctor immediately if you have extreme thirst, a dry mouth, warm, dry skin but no sweating, sleepiness or confusion, or blood sugar that's higher than 350 mg/dl. Blood sugar that's over 500 mg/dl is a medical emergency; call 911.

20 percent of them become legally blind within five years of diagnosis.

Because your vision can progressively worsen, it's crucial to visit an eye doctor for regular screening if you have diabetes. In addition to controlling your blood sugar, some conventional doctors also recommend a procedure called laser photocoagulation to burn and seal leaking blood vessels. Although this painless therapy doesn't usually improve eyesight, it can slow the rate of vision loss and prevent blindness.

Plus, research suggests that supplements of Pycnogenol, a pine bark extract that has antioxidant activity and helps support blood vessel walls, may reduce blood leakage and improve vision in people with diabetic retinopathy. Take 25 mg of Pycnogenol (available in health food stores) one to three times a day and give it a good two-month trial.

Glaucoma. High blood sugar levels can harm your eye's optic nerve, making people with diabetes twice as likely to develop glaucoma. In this condition, for unknown reasons, fluid in the eye drains too slowly, leading to higher pressure within the eye (intraocular pressure or IOP), which can damage the optic nerve and cause vision loss. As the disease progresses, you lose peripheral (side) vision first and central vision last. Conventional treatment usually involves prescription eye drops and drugs to control IOP, and the following natural measures may also help.

Watch your vices. Studies are mixed, but there's some evidence that smoking and consuming large amounts of caffeine could worsen glaucoma. That's because smokers have reduced blood flow to the eyes, which compounds damage to the optic nerve in people with glaucoma. Caffeine can also constrict blood vessels in the eye, with the same result.

Work it out. Although there are some concerns that physical activity might increase IOP, studies show that regular exercise is actually safe and beneficial for people with open-angle glaucoma. According to recent research, people with glaucoma who walk briskly or ride stationary bikes for 40 minutes at least four times a week can lower their IOP, in some cases enough to reduce their need for glaucoma medication. (Check with your doctor before starting an exercise program or decreasing your medications.)

Take antioxidants. Research suggests that glaucoma patients who supplement with very high doses of vitamin C (at least 2 grams daily) have lower IOP than those who do not.

Explore acupuncture. There's some evidence that people with glaucoma who receive acupuncture at various points on the body have significant decreases in their IOP after only one session.

Try ginkgo. Preliminary research suggests that people with glaucoma who supplement with ginkgo have a significant decrease in vision damage compared with those who don't take this herb, possibly because ginkgo increases blood flow to the eye. Take 40 mg of a standardized ginkgo extract three times a day and be aware that this herb can interact with Coumadin and other blood-thinning drugs.

Kidney Disease

When your kidneys' tiny blood vessels are damaged by high blood sugar, their ability to filter out waste is compromised, a condition known as nephropathy that affects up to 20 percent of people with diabetes. When renal organs have to work harder and harder to filter waste from the blood, they may eventually fail altogether. If that happens, you'll need to have your blood filtered by a machine (dialysis) or have a kidney transplant. Because kidney problems often have no symptoms, it's important for people with diabetes to see a doctor regularly, who can check for signs of this condition.

In addition to controlling your blood sugar, you can head off kidney damage by keeping your blood pressure low: Even a slight increase in blood pressure can cause kidney disease to worsen. You can control your blood pressure by exercising regularly, maintaining a healthy weight, not smoking, and consuming less salt in your diet. Your doctor may also prescribe certain medications to lower blood pressure. And your dietitian may suggest that you follow a low-protein diet, which is less taxing on the kidneys.

Memory Troubles

Research suggests that older people with diabetes face anywhere from a 9 to 65 percent higher risk of developing dementia and Alzheimer's disease than people without diabetes, although it's not clear why (nerve and blood vessel damage in the brain probably play a role). Until more is known, your best bet for warding off memory problems is to keep blood sugar levels under control and to stay mentally and physically active.

CHAPTER NINE

Living with Diabetes

iabetes doesn't just affect your body—it can also impact many different aspects of your life. From relationships with your spouse and family to the work you do to your travel plans, diabetes can present a number of challenging situations. Yet, having diabetes doesn't have to slow you down or cause you to shy away from certain activities. By planning ahead and making a few key adjustments, you can live an enjoyable and active life.

Diabetes: A Family Affair

Even though you're the one who has diabetes, this disease can influence other family members, too. They'll need to learn about the condition, understand how they can help you test blood sugar or treat hypoglycemia if necessary, and perhaps even change some of their own eating habits to accommodate your meal plans. This can make life easier for you—and for your loved ones, since involving them in your care can help alleviate any concerns they may have about the condition and your health. Plus, diabetes has a strong genetic link, so educating your family can make them more likely to notice the signs, symptoms, and risk factors for the disease in themselves. And studies have found that one of the best indications of how well someone takes care of their diabetes is the amount of support they receive from their family and friends. Here are some suggestions for helping each other cope with your diabetes.

Educate. If you feel like your loved ones just don't understand what it's like to have diabetes, you might be right. They may not be sure of how

> "Don't judge each day by the harvest you reap, but by the seeds you sow."
>
> ROBERT LOUIS STEVENSON

certain foods, activities, and stresses influence your blood sugar or why you need to take time out to test your glucose. Giving them this book is one way to educate friends and family, or you can show them some of the materials listed in the Resource Guide on page 74. Once they have a better grasp of what diabetes is and how it can affect you, they'll be more likely to understand how you're feeling.

Involve. When you have to change the foods you eat, it can impact your family's meals, too. This is easier if they're also willing to start eating healthy, but it's still a challenge nonetheless. To ease the transition, consider bringing your significant other along on visits to your certified diabetes educator (CDE) or dietitian, especially if he or she does most of the cooking or grocery shopping. By making your family a part of these changes, you'll set a good example and improve their health as well. The same goes for physical activity: Involve family members by going on walks or joining a health club together, for example.

Ask. It's likely that your loved ones want to help you cope with diabetes but don't know how to do so. Ask them directly for assistance, and give specific examples of how they can help. For instance, you might suggest that your spouse watch your children for a few minutes every evening while you check your blood sugar or do a progressive muscle relaxation exercise. Or ask your children to accompany you to the grocery store so they can help choose healthier foods they'll enjoy, too.

When Sex Is Less Desirable

Another way that diabetes can affect your relationships involves your sex life. Having this condition can affect your sexuality both physically and emotionally, making you either less interested in or less able to enjoy sex. As you learned in Chapter Eight, high blood sugar can cause blood vessels to harden and narrow. In men, this may reduce blood flow to the penis, leading to erectile dysfunction (impotence). In women, decreased blood flow or nerve damage to the genitals can cause vaginal dryness, decreased sensitivity, and difficulty achieving orgasm, while high blood sugar can increase the risk of yeast infections. Emotions like depression and anxiety, or self-esteem issues tied to diabetes, can interfere with your desire for sex as well.

Fortunately, keeping blood sugar levels close to normal may improve sexual function in both men and women. If you do find yourself dealing with one of the physical or emotional causes of sexual dysfunction mentioned here, see your doctor, who may be able to prescribe medications or suggest counseling to better cope with these problems. By the way, some people worry that the physical exertion of sex will trigger an episode of hypoglycemia (low blood sugar). But, when it comes to diabetes, sex isn't really any different than any other physical activity. Stave off any problems by treating sex the way you would exercise: Eat about an hour before sexual activity, check your blood sugar before and afterward, and adjust your insulin dose if necessary.

Diabetes on the Job

Whether or not you decide to tell your employer that you have diabetes is up to you. You may wish to keep your diabetes private or might worry how your colleagues will treat you if they know. On the other hand, it's helpful if at least a few of your coworkers know what to do in case you have a diabetes-related emergency. And if you need special accommodations, such as short breaks to check your blood sugar or adjustments to your work schedule, you'll need to tell your boss. (The Americans with Disabilities Act requires employers to make such "reasonable accommodations" for people with diabetes.)

Coping with diabetes can be tougher in some workplaces than others. If you work at a typical 9-to-5 desk job, you might not need to make many changes at all. But if you're on your feet all day, have a hard time taking breaks, or work unpredictable, night, or "swing" shifts, it can be harder to control diabetes. First, talk to your doctor or CDE, who can suggest adjustments to your treatment: Maybe you'll need to change the times or doses of insulin you take, for example. And if you've made your boss aware that you have diabetes, he or she can help you brainstorm some ideas involving shifts, breaks, or other ways to meet your medical needs.

On the Go: Traveling with Diabetes

Diabetes might seem like a constant companion, but having this condition doesn't have to stop you from seeing the world. Whether you're touring Europe or spending a week at the beach, you can do almost anything—you'll just need to do a little more planning than most other travelers. Here are some tips for having a safe trip.

Get it in writing. Before you leave, ask your doctor to write a letter

Q&A

Is it safe for women with diabetes to get pregnant?

In the past, high blood sugar put a pregnant woman with diabetes at higher risk of having a miscarriage, stillbirth, or baby with birth defects. Today, having a baby can still place extra strains on your body and requires you to control your diabetes very carefully. And babies born to women with diabetes do have a greater chance of having a higher birth weight, which may require you to have a C-section. Still, it is possible for you to get pregnant and have a healthy pregnancy and baby if you have diabetes.

As with many other aspects of having this condition, it's best to plan ahead if you have diabetes and want to have a child. Start with a visit to your doctor about three to six months before you start trying to conceive to have your A1C, blood pressure, heart, kidneys, nerves, and eyes checked or tested. It's also important to discuss the effects of pregnancy on your diabetes, since some complications, like retinopathy and neuropathy, can worsen with pregnancy. If you currently take diabetes medications, your doctor will likely switch you to insulin, since oral drugs haven't yet been proven to be safe for expectant moms. Plus, you may want to check with your dietitian to review your meal plan. That might seem like a lot of work, but for many women, being pregnant can be the best motivator of all to keep diabetes under control.

explaining that you have diabetes and what medications you take to treat it. You can show this letter to airport security if they question your need for lancets or syringes, for example. Also, plan to carry a prescription for your insulin or diabetes drugs: You may need it if you lose or run out of your current medications while on vacation.

Plan ahead. If you'll be crossing time zones, talk to your doctor or CDE about when you should take your insulin shots or oral medications. If you're visiting a foreign country, you might also learn how to say, "I have diabetes" or "Sugar or juice, please" in that language in case of an emergency.

Pack wisely. You should pack at least twice as much diabetes medication and testing supplies as you think you will need on your trip and store half of them in your carry-on bag. If you're flying, keep your medications or insulin and syringes in their original packaging if possible, along with the prescription label from your drugstore. (You must also be carrying insulin to be allowed to bring syringes through airport security.) For domestic flights, you can bring lancets on board a plane as long as they are capped and accompanied by a glucose meter that has the manufacturer's name on it; call ahead if you're taking an international flight to ask about the airline's specific rules and regulations. No matter how you travel, you'll also want to pack comfortable shoes, wear your medical alert bracelet, and bring a snack like dried fruit, nuts, or crackers and peanut butter, plus some quick-acting glucose tablets or hard candy in case of low blood sugar.

Fly right. Call your airline in advance to request a special meal for people with diabetes. During long flights (or drives), try to get up or get out of the car and periodically stretch your legs to avoid developing dangerous blood clots.

Staying Safe When You're Sick

Feeling under the weather has special implications for people with diabetes. When you've got a cold, the flu, or an infection, feel nauseated or are vomiting, are recovering from surgery, or have any type of injury, your blood sugar may be higher than usual, even if you're eating less. That's because insulin is often less effective during illness. It's best to create a "sick day" action plan with your doctor or CDE in advance so that you can discuss the following tips and include any additional advice they might have.

Stay on schedule. Take your usual medication or insulin shots, even if you can't eat. Check your blood sugar more often than usual—every three to four hours all day and night—and have someone do it for you if you cannot; keep track of these readings in your log.

Keep hydrated. You should try to drink about 6 to 8 ounces of water, decaffeinated tea or diet soda, or broth every hour that you're awake, since dehydration can increase your risk of developing hyperosmolar hyperglycemic state, or HHS (see page 60). If you can't eat, alternate sugary products (such as apple juice or decaffeinated soda) with sugar-free drinks every other hour to keep your blood sugar from falling too low.

When in doubt, ask. Some cough and cold medications contain alcohol, sugar, or the drug pseudoephedrine (which can raise blood pressure), so check with your doctor or pharmacist before taking them. Plus, call your doctor if you have vomiting or diarrhea or blood sugar that stays above 250 mg/dl for at least two checks.

CHAPTER TEN

New Research on the Horizon

ith each chapter of this book, you've found plenty of good tips for lowering your blood sugar and controlling diabetes. But you may still wonder whether researchers will ever find a way to completely eradicate this chronic disease. Unfortunately, there's no cure on the immediate horizon, says Duke University endocrinologist Mark Feinglos, MD. So you need to use the lifestyle measures, medications, supplements, and other therapies discussed in this guide in order to control the disease.

Meanwhile, researchers are hard at work looking for new ways to diagnose diabetes and developing better treatments for it. To learn more about the latest state of the science, *Self Healing* spoke to Mary Elizabeth Patti, MD, a research investigator at the Joslin Diabetes Center and assistant professor of medicine at Harvard Medical School. Dr. Patti and her colleagues are particularly interested in finding the genes and other markers that will help identify people who are most at risk for diabetes, while other researchers are continuing to study the effects of diet, exercise, and other lifestyle measures to determine the best treatment strategies. Here are five areas of diabetes research that you'll likely hear more about over the next several years.

Risk identification. Preventing diabetes and treating it early will become easier once doctors can better pinpoint those people at highest risk. Researchers have found that in people with diabetes, certain genes that regulate the number and function of mitochondria (the structures in cells that make energy from carbohydrates, fat, and protein) are "turned off," which stops the mitochondria from producing energy the way they should. When mitochondria can't properly burn fat, it builds up in muscle cells, promot-

> "Experience is not what happens to you; it's what you do with what happens to you."
>
> ALDOUS HUXLEY

ing insulin resistance. This process may also cause weight gain, which further contributes to insulin resistance and eventually diabetes.

Although their research is still in its early stages, Dr. Patti and her colleagues hope to someday use this knowledge to check blood samples for genes, proteins, and other markers that behave differently in people prone to diabetes. That means that someone susceptible to the disease (who has a family history of diabetes, for example) could learn exactly *how* high his or her risk is through a simple blood test at the doctor's office—even before symptoms or insulin resistance occur.

Targeted prevention programs. "We're developing more and more powerful techniques to understand the biology of diabetes," Dr. Patti says. "The key is to translate this into prevention." Research such as the Diabetes Prevention Program study has already shown that a combination of healthy eating, regular exercise, and just a small amount of weight loss can reduce the odds of diabetes by almost 60 percent (oral diabetes drugs like metformin can also lower risk, although to a lesser degree). Dr. Patti believes such prevention measures need to be implemented as soon as possible. By identifying people at risk even earlier with the techniques discussed above, doctors will be able to start them on a lifestyle program for diabetes prevention even before they develop prediabetes.

To reverse the growing epidemic of diabetes, we'll need to take the right steps to stay healthy as a society, from increasing physical education classes in schools to decreasing suburban "sprawl" that leads to communities without sidewalks for walking and encourages residents to drive everywhere. "Diabetes is a critical public health problem," says Dr. Patti. "We *all* need to do our part to prevent it, from government health programs to researchers to community planners."

Personalized treatment plans. Although doctors and dietitians currently adapt diabetes treatments to patients' individual needs, another important goal is to be able to create a truly personalized plan for patients. After diagnosing people with diabetes or prediabetes, Dr. Patti believes, physicians could determine the best treatment based on their individual genetic markers. Currently, this approach is used by oncologists for some forms of cancer: They recommend specific chemotherapy drugs based on individual proteins, genes, and other markers in tumors. In the future, Dr. Patti hopes that diabetes treatment will move in the same direction.

Dietary approaches. According to Dr. Patti, there's renewed interest and greater acceptance in the medical community of various food compounds and their effect on diabetes. She expects that we'll see more research in the coming years on the value of the spice cinnamon (see page 27) and the mineral chromium (page 50) in lowering blood sugar, for example. Plus, researchers hope to clarify the impact of different diets (low-fat, low-carbohydrate, and others).

No more needles. Researchers are working on new ways of testing blood sugar levels without needles, possibly by using ultrasound, radio waves, and beams of light applied to the skin. Plus, they're creating new medical devices for delivering insulin to the body without syringes: Approaches under development include insulin that can be taken as pills, as a nasal or oral spray, and as a skin patch.

While such research is promising, it may take years before the results can actually be applied to people with diabetes. In the meantime, managing your weight, eating well, and getting regular physical activity have been shown in many studies to lower blood sugar, points out Dr. Patti, and their benefits are crystal clear. You can also follow the stress reduction exercises, supplement recommendations, and conventional treatment advice in this book to lower blood sugar and prevent diabetes complications. Stay on top of the latest research by reading information from the Joslin Diabetes Center, American Diabetes Association, and other organizations listed in the Resource Guide (page 74) and then discussing it with your doctor. Remember, there's a lot you can do to help yourself live a long and healthy life with diabetes.

Diabetes Treatment Summary

To help start you on your way to controlling blood sugar levels, here's an at-a-glance compilation of Dr. Weil's best advice for treating diabetes.

KEY

★ Dr. Weil's top recommendations

✔ Other approaches worth trying

Conventional Treatment

★ Assemble a "health care team" that includes your primary care physician (or endocrinologist), a certified diabetes educator, and a dietitian. You may also want to see other health professionals as various needs arise.

★ Get screened regularly for vision difficulties, foot problems, heart disease, and other diabetes-related complications.

★ Take oral diabetes medications or use insulin if needed.

Self-Care

★ Test your blood sugar at home as recommended by your doctor and keep track of these readings in a daily log.

★ Check your feet daily for blisters, cuts, abrasions, and other injuries.

Diet

★ See a registered dietitian for advice on designing a meal plan that meets your individual needs and helps you lose to weight if needed. A dietitian can also explain valuable meal planning skills like carbohydrate counting and the glycemic index.

★ Get about 45 to 50 percent of your daily calories from carbohydrates. Favor complex carbs like whole grains and legumes, and keep your consumption of sugar and refined carbohydrates to a minimum.

★ Get about 25 to 35 percent of your daily calories from fat. Eat fewer saturated and trans fats and opt for more monounsaturated fats (in olive oil and some nuts) and omega-3 fatty acids (in flax, walnuts, and oily, cold-water fish like salmon and sardines).

★ Get 15 to 20 percent of your daily calories from protein, and choose fish and healthier plant-based proteins like soy and other beans over animal protein.

★ Eat more high-fiber foods, like whole grains, legumes, nuts, fruits, and vegetables.

✔ Ask your dietitian whether or not alcoholic and caffeinated beverages will fit into your meal plan.

✔ Consider adding cinnamon to your meals—this spice may lower blood sugar.

Physical Activity

★ Check with your physician before beginning an exercise program. Be sure to test your blood sugar before and after exercising.

★ Get regular aerobic activity (walking, cycling, swimming, etc.) for 20 to 60 minutes at least three times a week.

★ Strength train two or three times a week.

★ Practice flexibility and balance exercises, like yoga, tai chi, or stretching, at least two or three days a week.

✔ Use a pedometer to monitor and increase your physical activity.

Weight Control

★ Achieve and maintain a healthy weight:

- Identify proper portions of food and drink, and make a conscious effort to reduce your portion sizes.

- Keep a food diary for a few weeks or more by recording every food and beverage you consume, the portion size, when you consumed it, and how hungry you were at the time. Calculate your daily calories to become more aware of your intake.

- Learn to eat mindfully and slowly by focusing on your meal with no outside distractions like TV or reading material.

- Be physically active on a regular basis (see above).

Stress Reduction

★ Practice progressive muscle relaxation, breath work, or another relaxation technique regularly.

✔ See a mental health professional if you need help coping with anger, depression, or other negative emotions.

Supplements

Note: It is safe, but not necessary, to use all of these supplements at the same time.

★ Take up to 400 mg of alpha-lipoic acid daily, or 800 mg if you have neuropathy.

★ Take up to 1,000 mcg of glucose tolerance factor (GTF) chromium daily.

★ Take 200 to 600 mg of American ginseng daily before meals. Look for products standardized for ginsenosides, the active ingredient.

★ Take 400 mg of magnesium daily, unless you have kidney problems. Taking this mineral with twice as much calcium will help neutralize its laxative effect.

★ Take 400 to 800 IU of natural vitamin E (or 80 mg of mixed tocopherols and tocotrienols) daily as part of an antioxidant regimen.

✔ Experiment with one or more of the herbal remedies listed on page 53 and 54 if desired.

Acknowledgements

Dr. Andrew Weil's Self Healing would like to thank the following people for their valuable expertise and assistance with this special report:

Jenny Catherine Eriksen, Media Relations and Communications Coordinator at the Joslin Diabetes Center in Boston, Massachusetts

Mark Feinglos, MD, Professor of Medicine and Chief of the Division of Endocrinology, Metabolism and Nutrition at Duke University Medical Center in Durham, North Carolina

Randy Horwitz, MD, PhD, Medical Director of the Program in Integrative Medicine, University of Arizona in Tucson

Mary Elizabeth Patti, MD, Assistant Investigator at the Section on Cellular and Molecular Physiology, Joslin Diabetes Center and Assistant Professor of Medicine at Harvard Medical School in Boston, Massachusetts

Jo-Anne Rizzotto, MEd, RD, LDN, CDE, Curriculum Development and Implementation Specialist at the Joslin Clinic in Boston, Massachusetts

Victoria Rommel, MD, Anson Family Medicine, Wadesboro, North Carolina

Richard S. Surwit, PhD, ABPP, FAClinP, Professor and Chief, Division of Medical Psychology and Vice Chairman for Research at the Department of Psychiatry and Behavioral Sciences at Duke University Medical Center in Durham, North Carolina

Kirsten Ward, MS, RCEP, CDE, exercise physiologist and Latino Program Coordinator at the Joslin Clinic in Boston, Massachusetts

Resource Guide

General Information

ORGANIZATIONS

American Diabetes Association
ATTN: National Call Center
1701 North Beauregard Street
Alexandria, VA 22311
(800) 342-2383
www.diabetes.org

This national nonprofit organization offers the latest information on diabetes research and sells diabetes-related publications. Their website provides recipes for healthy meals, simple exercises to get fit, and listings of local ADA events.

Joslin Diabetes Center
One Joslin Place
Boston, MA 02215
(617) 732-2400
www.joslin.org

The world's leading diabetes center is affiliated with Harvard Medical School and offers online and live classes, support groups, and discussion boards on their website, as well as a selection of publications, videos, and other educational resources that you can purchase. The Joslin Clinic also has more than 20 affiliated centers nationwide.

National Diabetes Information Clearinghouse
One Information Way
Bethesda, MD 20892-3560
(800) 860-8747
http://diabetes.niddk.nih.gov/intro/index.htm

A service of the National Institutes of Health's National Institute of Diabetes and Digestive and Kidney Diseases, this clearinghouse offers the public basic information on diabetes control, prevention, and treatment, some of which is available in Spanish.

American Association of Diabetes Educators
100 W. Monroe Street, Suite 400
Chicago, IL 60603
(800) 338-3633
www.aadenet.org

This professional organization provides some general diabetes information to the public. Its website includes a searchable database to help patients locate certified diabetes educators nationwide.

BOOKS

American Diabetes Association Complete Guide to Diabetes
(Bantam, 2003)

This sourcebook from the ADA discusses oral medications and insulin, dieting, exercise, coping with diabetes at school and work, and more.

Diabetes for Dummies
Alan L. Rubin, MD (For Dummies, 1999)

This simplified summary explains what you need to know about living with diabetes and is a good resource for people newly diagnosed with the condition.

The Diabetes Problem Solver: Quick Answers to Your Questions about Treatment and Self-Care
Nancy Touchette, PhD (American Diabetes Association, 1999)

This dictionary-style reference covers the causes of and solutions for diabetic complications. Special sections on problems particular to men, women, and children are included.

The Everything Diabetes Book
Paula Ford-Martin with Ian Blumer, MD (Adams Media Corporation, 2004)

Simple and reader-friendly, this book covers everything from the causes of diabetes and treatments for complications to tips for living, working, and traveling with the disease.

A Field Guide to Type 2 Diabetes
(American Diabetes Association, 2004)

This handy pocket reference includes medical guidelines, treatment goals, and stories from other people with diabetes.

The First Year—Type 2 Diabetes: An Essential Guide for the Newly Diagnosed
Gretchen Becker (Marlowe & Company, 2001)

From a health writer who also has diabetes, this book helps guide the newly diagnosed patient through 12 months with the condition.

The Uncomplicated Guide to Diabetes Complications, Second Edition

Marvin E. Levin, MD, and Michael A. Pfeifer, MD (American Diabetes Association, 2002)

This guide helps you to understand the complications of diabetes, from minor infections to cardiovascular disease.

OTHER

Diabetes Forecast

The leading monthly diabetes magazine for over 50 years contains the latest information and tips for coping with the condition; a subscription is included with a paid membership to the American Diabetes Association.

Exercise and Diabetes

BOOKS

Diabetes: Your Complete Exercise Guide

Neil F. Gordon, MD, PhD (Human Kinetics Publishers, 1993)

Offers a clear explanation of the different types of diabetes, four complete exercise programs, and guidelines for safe exercise.

The Diabetic Athlete

Sheri Colberg, PhD (Human Kinetics Publishers, 2000)

Written by a diabetic athlete, this book gives insights and advice on controlling your diabetes while training and competing in various sports and activities.

The "I Hate to Exercise" Book for People with Diabetes

Charlotte Hayes (American Diabetes Association, 2001)

Find out how to turn everyday activities into fitness opportunities to help control your diabetes.

Small Steps, Big Rewards Book and Pedometer Package

(American Diabetes Association, 2003)

This book helps you turn a daily walk into a life-changing fitness program, and the kit includes a pedometer to use during your workouts to count your every step.

VIDEOS

Keep Moving . . . Keep Healthy with Diabetes

This first-of-its-kind low impact exercise video created by the Joslin Diabetes Center includes seated and standing workouts for those with and without physical limitations. You can purchase it from www.joslin.org.

Nutrition and Diabetes

BOOKS

The Commonsense Guide to Weight Loss for People with Diabetes

Barbara Caleen Hansen, PhD, and Shauna S. Roberts, PhD (American Diabetes Association, 1998)

This book helps people with diabetes to lose weight and keep it off with a healthy lifestyle.

The Diabetes Food & Nutrition Bible

Hope S. Warshaw and Robyn Webb (American Diabetes Association, 2001)

A nutrition guide and cookbook in one to help you eat the foods that will heal your body and keep your blood sugar levels stable.

The Joslin Diabetes Quick and Easy Cookbook

Frances T. Giedt and Bonnie S. Polin, PhD (Fireside, 1998)

Two hundred delicious, easy-to-prepare recipes for people with diabetes from the nutritional services staff of the Joslin Diabetes Center.

The New Glucose Revolution

Jennie Brand-Miller, PhD (Marlowe & Company, 2002)

Learn how to use the glycemic index to influence blood sugar with this comprehensive book.

101 Nutrition Tips for People with Diabetes

Patti B. Geil and Lea Ann Holzmeister (American Diabetes Association, 1999)

This book offer tips and techniques on nutrition, weight loss, meal planning, and more.

The Other Diabetes: Living and Eating Well with Type 2 Diabetes

Elizabeth N. Hiser (Morrow Cookbooks, 2002)

A nutritionist offers tasty, safe, and healthy dietary advice for people with diabetes.

Stress Reduction and Diabetes

BOOKS

The Mind-Body Diabetes Revolution
Richard S. Surwit, PhD, with Alisa Bauman (Free Press, 2004)
This book explains how stress-reduction techniques and other mind-body approaches can help control diabetes.

Progressive Relaxation: A Self-Training Program
Richard S. Surwit, PhD (available from www.richardsurwit.com)
This CD and instruction manual explain how to use progressive muscle relaxation exercises to control your glucose levels.

Zen and the Art of Diabetes Maintenance
Charles Creekmore (American Diabetes Association, 2002)
This book includes expert advice on the healing power of spiritual practice and stories from people with diabetes.

Pregnancy and Diabetes

BOOKS

Diabetes & Pregnancy: What to Expect, Fourth Edition
(American Diabetes Association, 2001)
This guide shows expectant mothers how to have a healthy baby, from planning a pregnancy to labor and delivery. Includes information on insulin, nutrition, complications, exercise, and more.

OTHER

Sweet Success Program
www.llu.edu/llumc/sweetsuccess
The program provides information and health care to pregnant women with diabetes living in California. Free educational materials are available to pregnant women throughout the country at their website.

Selected References

Below, you'll find selected citations for studies, books, and other published material used in researching and writing this guide. In addition, *Self Healing* relied on information from organizations such as those mentioned in the Resource Guide (see page 74), interviews with physicians and other health experts, and Dr. Weil's own experience in treating patients with diabetes. The list that follows is a selective and by no means complete listing of all references used in this book.

Chapter One: Diabetes 101

American Diabetes Association Complete Guide to Diabetes (Bantam, 2003).

The Everything Diabetes Book (Ford-Martin, Paula, et al.; Adams Media Corporation, 2004).

A Field Guide to Type 2 Diabetes (American Diabetes Association, 2004).

New York Times, October 8, 2002. "Women Can Fight an Almost Secret Syndrome."

New York Times, December 23, 2003. "Stampede of Diabetes as US Races to Obesity."

Postgraduate Medicine, April 1997; 101(4). "From ants to analogues: Puzzles and promises in diabetes management."

Time, November 30, 2003. "Why So Many of Us Are Getting Diabetes."

Chapter Two: Conventional Treatment

American Diabetes Association Complete Guide to Diabetes (Bantam, 2003).

The Everything Diabetes Book (Ford-Martin, Paula, et al.; Adams Media Corporation, 2004).

The First Year—Type 2 Diabetes: An Essential Guide for the Newly Diagnosed (Becker, Gretchen; Marlowe & Company, 2001).

"7 Principles for Controlling Your Diabetes for Life" (National Diabetes Education Program, 2001).

Chapter Three: Healthy Eating for Diabetes

Alternative Therapies in Health and Medicine, November/December 2003; 9(6): 24–32. "An Integrative Approach to the Management of Type 2 Diabetes Mellitus."

American Diabetes Association Complete Guide to Diabetes (Bantam, 2003).

American Journal of Clinical Nutrition, August 2002; 76(2): 390–8. "Whole-grain intake is favorably associated with metabolic risk factors for type 2 diabetes and cardiovascular disease in the Framingham Offspring Study."

American Journal of Public Health, September 2000; 90(9): 1409–15. "A prospective study of whole-grain intake and risk of type 2 diabetes mellitus in US women."

Circulation, August 1, 2000; 102(5): 494–9. "Moderate alcohol consumption and risk of coronary heart disease among women with type 2 diabetes mellitus."

Diabetes Care, January 2003; 26 Supplement 1: S51-61. "Evidence-based nutrition principles and recommendations for the treatment and prevention of diabetes and related complications."

Diabetes Care, February 2004; 27(2): 538–46. "Carbohydrate nutrition, insulin resistance, and the prevalence of the metabolic syndrome in the Framingham Offspring Cohort."

Diabetes Care, June 2004; 27(6): 1281–5. "High-fiber cereal reduces postprandial insulin responses in hyperinsulinemic but not normo-insulinemic subjects."

Diabetes Care, August 2004; 27(8): 2047–8. "Caffeine impairs glucose metabolism in type 2 diabetes."

Diabetes Spectrum, January 2002; 15(1): 11–4. "Diabetes Bars and Beverages: The Benefits and the Controversies."

Environmental Nutrition, July 2003. "The 'Diabetic Diet' Comes of Age: New Research Focuses on Foods."

The Everything Diabetes Book (Ford-Martin, Paula, et al.; Adams Media Corporation, 2004).

The First Year—Type 2 Diabetes: An Essential Guide for the Newly Diagnosed (Becker, Gretchen; Marlowe & Company, 2001).

Journal of the American Dietetic Association, April 2004; 104(4): 560–66. "Food habits are related to glycemic control among people with type 2 diabetes mellitus."

Journal of the American Medical Association, May 15, 2002; 287(19): 2559–62. "Effects of moderate alcohol intake on fasting insulin and glucose concentrations and insulin sensitivity in postmenopausal women: a randomized controlled trial."

Journal of the American Medical Association, November 27, 2002; 288(20): 2554–60. "Nut and peanut butter consumption and risk of type 2 diabetes in women."

Journal of the American Medical Association, March 10, 2004; 291(10): 1213–9. "Coffee consumption and risk of type 2 diabetes mellitus among middle-aged Finnish men and women."

The Lancet, November 9, 2002; 360(9344): 1477–8. "Coffee consumption and risk of type 2 diabetes mellitus."

Chapter Four: Staying Fit with Diabetes

American Diabetes Association Complete Guide to Diabetes (Bantam, 2003).

Clinical Diabetes, July–August 1997. "Use of exercise in the treatment of type 2 diabetes mellitus."

Diabetes Care, March 2003; 26(3): 944–5. "Does exercise without weight loss improve insulin sensitivity?"

The Everything Diabetes Book (Ford-Martin, Paula, et al.; Adams Media Corporation, 2004).

Healing Moves (Krucoff, Carol, et al.; Three Rivers Press, 2001).

The Physician and Sportsmedicine, April 1999; 4(27). "Exercise in Diabetes Management."

The Physician and Sportsmedicine, April 1999; 4(27). "Exercising with Diabetes."

The Physician and Sportsmedicine, April 2000; 28(4). "Exercise and Diabetes Control."

The Physician and Sportsmedicine, January 2004; 32(1). "Physical Activity and Type 2 Diabetes."

The Uncomplicated Guide to Diabetes Complications (Levin, MD, Marvin E., et al.; American Diabetes Association, 2002).

Chapter Five: Controlling Your Weight

American Diabetes Association Complete Guide to Diabetes (Bantam, 2003).

Diabetes, September 2004; 53: 2375–82. "Effect of a high-protein, low-carbohydrate diet on blood glucose control in people with type 2 diabetes."

Diabetes Care, February 2002; 25(2): 397–8. "Is weight loss a cure for type 2 diabetes?"

Diabetes Care, March 2004; 27(3): 657–62. "Trying to lose weight, losing weight, and 9-year mortality in overweight US adults with diabetes."

The First Year—Type 2 Diabetes: An Essential Guide for the Newly Diagnosed (Becker, Gretchen; Marlowe & Company, 2001).

New England Journal of Medicine, February 7, 2002; 346(6): 393–403. "Reduction in the incidence of type 2 diabetes with lifestyle intervention or metformin."

New England Journal of Medicine, June 17, 2004; 350(25): 2549–57. "Absence of an effect of liposuction on insulin action and risk factors for coronary heart disease."

Chapter Six: Stress Less

American Diabetes Association Complete Guide to Diabetes (Bantam, 2003).

Annals of Internal Medicine, October 15, 1998; 129(8): 613–21. "Cognitive behavioral therapy for depression in type 2 diabetes mellitus. A randomized, controlled trial."

Diabetes Care, January 2002; 25(1): 30–4. "Stress management improves long-term glycemic control in type 2 diabetes."

Duke Health Brief, April 1, 2004. "Using the mind to fight diabetes."

The Everything Diabetes Book (Ford-Martin, Paula, et al.; Adams Media Corporation, 2004)

The First Year—Type 2 Diabetes: An Essential Guide for the Newly Diagnosed (Becker, Gretchen; Marlowe & Company, 2001).

General Hospital Psychiatry, September 1998; 20(5): 305–6. "Predicting response to cognitive behavior therapy of depression in type 2 diabetes."

The Mind-Body Diabetes Revolution (Surwit, PhD, Richard S., et al.; Free Press, 2004).

The Uncomplicated Guide to Diabetes Complications (Levin, MD, Marvin E., et al.; American Diabetes Association, 2002).

Chapter Seven: Selecting Supplements

Alternative Medicine Review, February 2002; 7(1): 45–58. "Alternative therapies for type 2 diabetes."

Alternative Medicine Review, February 2003; 8(1): 20–7. "Therapeutic applications of fenugreek."

Alternative Therapies in Health and Medicine, November/ December 2003; 9(6): 24–32. "An Integrative Approach to the Management of Type 2 Diabetes."

Archives of Internal Medicine, April 10, 2000; 160(7): 1009–13. "American ginseng (*Panax quinquefolius* L) reduces postprandial glycemia in nondiabetic subjects and subjects with type 2 diabetes mellitus."

Diabetes Care, April 2003; 26(4): 1277–94. "Systematic review of herbs and dietary supplements for glycemic control in diabetes."

Diabetes Care, February 2004; 27(2): 436–40. "Efficacy of *Ipomoea batatas* (Caiapo) on diabetes control in type 2 diabetic subjects treated with diet."

Integrative Medicine (Rakel, MD, David; Elsevier Science, 2002), p. 233–41.

Treatment of Diabetes with Natural Therapeutics, Third Edition (National Diabetes Fund, September 2002).

Chapter Eight: Coping with Complications

American Diabetes Association Complete Guide to Diabetes (Bantam, 2003).

Diabetes Care, November 2003; 26(11): 2999-3005. "Complications in young adults with early-onset type 2 diabetes: losing the relative protection of youth."

The Everything Diabetes Book (Ford-Martin, Paula, et al.; Adams Media Corporation, 2004).

The Uncomplicated Guide to Diabetes Complications (Levin, MD, Marvin E., et al.; American Diabetes Association, 2002).

Chapter Nine: Living with Diabetes

American Diabetes Association Complete Guide to Diabetes (Bantam, 2003).

The Everything Diabetes Book (Ford-Martin, Paula, et al.; Adams Media Corporation, 2004).

A Field Guide to Type 2 Diabetes (American Diabetes Association, 2004).

Chapter Ten: New Research

Interview with Mary Elizabeth Patti, MD, August 26, 2004.

Index